AT HOME IN EARLIER MT. PLEASANT MICHIGAN

A VISIT WITH OUR NEIGHBORS OF THE PAST

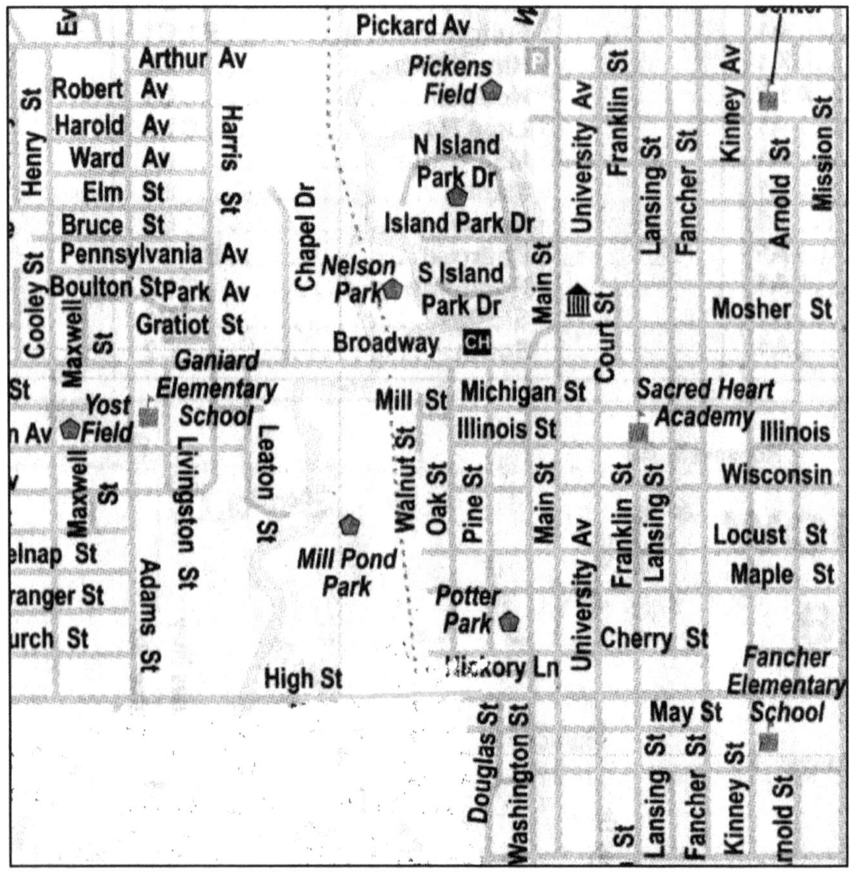

Area covered in this book: City of Mt. Pleasant, Michigan Due to space limitations, the perimeters covered in this book are for the most part, from Pickard Street on the north; Bellows Street on the south; Mission Street on the East and Walnut Street on the west. A small representation of the far West Side (west of the Chippewa Street to Henry Street) is included, in deference to Valerie Wolters upcoming book on the history of the Mt. Pleasants West Side.

ON THE COVERS:

FRONT COVER: *A portrait by Mt. Pleasant artist David Ellis, overlain by a period photo, of 711 South Fancher, see page 130.*

BACK COVER: *Period pictures overlaying a modern picture of 601 North Kinney Street, see page 42.*

AT HOME IN EARLIER MT. PLEASANT MICHIGAN

A VISIT WITH OUR NEIGHBORS OF THE PAST

Jack R. Westbrook

ORSB PUBLISHING
Mt. Pleasant, Michigan

ISBN: 10- 0984036113
LCCN: 2012916939
ISBN 13/EAN 13 978-0-9840361-1-0
Published by ORSB Publishing
POB 16 Mount Pleasant, Michigan, 48804-0016
989-773-5741

First Printing September, 2012
Second Printing October, 2012
Third Printing Novemberr, 2012

This book is especially dedicated to two premier Mt. Pleasant historians:

Isaac A. Fancher September 20, 1833-March 10, 1934, who spent 71 of his 101 years as a Mt. Pleasant resident; first formally platting the settlement in 1863 and serving its best interests as attorney, civic leader, Mayor, State Representative, and historian for the next seven decades. Fancher's 1911 Past and Present of Isabella County, Michigan book is the touchstone for all later area historians.

John Cumming, Director Emeritus of the Clarke Historical Library on the Mt. Pleasant campus of Central Michigan University. John's several books but particularly *This Place Mt. Pleasant* and *The First Hundred Years: A Portrait of Central Michigan University 1892-1992*, have become much-used tools in this author's attempts at later histories.

Also dedicated to anyone who ever wondered:

"What's the story on that (or my) house? I wonder who lived here before", and to those young and old with a passion for local history.

CONTENTS

Acknowledgements

Like my previous local photo histories, this is not my book.

It is our community telling of its story.

I am merely the assembly and package guy. Those people who were able to furnish photos are acknowledged in the photo credit page at the end of the book. To those who furnished stories, leads and encouragement, accept my deepest thanks. To that legion of people who have begun to seek me out by e-mail, phone and in person in places ranging from the supermarket to the aisles of the church to tell their family's stories, all are greatly appreciated and if not used by me, will be placed somewhere future researchers can find them.

Thanks to Sharon Brown, Isabella County Register of Deeds and her staff, Karen Jackson, Minde Lux, Betty Wright and Brent Ebright for their help, patience, and cooperation in availability of computer time allowing me to wend my way through the litany of property ownership of the homes in this book.

Thanks to Dave Rowley and Diane Adams in the Mt. Pleasant City Assessors office for their cooperation in making information and maps available that enabled me to create Appendix 1, Original Plat and Additions to the City of Mt. Pleasant contained in this book.

Thanks to my wife, Mary Lou, who supported me through this project.

Thanks to friend, genealogist, and co-author of another book Sherry Sponseller, whose research help was invaluable, as is that of the Mt. Pleasant Family History Center, Donna Hoff-Grambau. The next generation of the Sheery Sponseller family also needs a huge Thank you …. To Michelle Sponseller for her boundless knowledge of residential house types and architecture and here seminal work in identifying many local examples.

A special hats off to Loren Anderson, for his database of historic downtown Mt. Pleasnt businesses was invaluable in finding ouit where many of these folks of the past did business.

Thanks to both the Clarke Historical Library and the Mt. Pleasant Veterans Memorial Library for their splendid work in creating and maintaining the Isabella County Obituary Index online, on microfilm, and in card form at the Clarke.

Speaking of the Clarke, as always, thanks to Director Frank Boles, Archivist John Fierst, Bryan Whitledge, and Pat Thelan of Clarke Historical Library on the Mt. Pleasant campus of Central Michigan University for another fine job in helping locate microfilms and files, as well as scanning photos necessary to complete this job.

Introduction

The story of how the book came about can be found on page 35 describing the late Sher Muszynski's home at 721 North Fancher. This book came about due to the popularity of the Mt. Pleasant homes in my book *BIG Pictuire Book of Mt. Pleasant Michigan*. Some make encore appreances here.

For two years I, along with Mary Lou, my stalwart researcher, proofreader, driver, best friend and wife of more than five decades, have been combing the streets of Mt. Pleasant's historic core taking pictures of homes.

Our range of focus for this book was the historical core of town for the most part. A chapter called The Far West Side is added to include a few homes west of the Chippewa River, a part of town added as the town spread across the river and bridge traffic improved. That part of town will be explored more thoroughly in Valerie Wolter's upcoming book on the history of the West Side.

Next came the tedious task of sorting the nearly 600 photo result into something managable. First consideration was age, second was distinctive architectural design and the third was who lived there. A lesser fourth consideration was the research materials were available. For two months early this year I set up shop each Tuesday at the Isabella County Commission on Aging Mt. Pleasant building and Veterans Memorial Library where people brought photos and stories, of homes in the area of interest.

Details of the homes and their occupants, past and present, are from information gleaned from city directories, telephone books, the City of Mt. Pleasant Assessors Office and the Isabella County Register of Deeds. All are public record and any inaccuracies in translation of that material are mine. Final selection of houses for inclusion was purely random, recognizing it would be impossible to include all. Apologies if your house is left out. Some photos are third generation reprints but are included because of quality of content, if not appearance.

For those bent on continuing and filling the gaps in this work, research materials for this book, incuding houses not contained herein, are available at the Clarke Historical Library on the Mt. Pleasant Campus of Central Michigan University.

J.R.W. Mt. Pleasant, Michigan, August 25, 2012

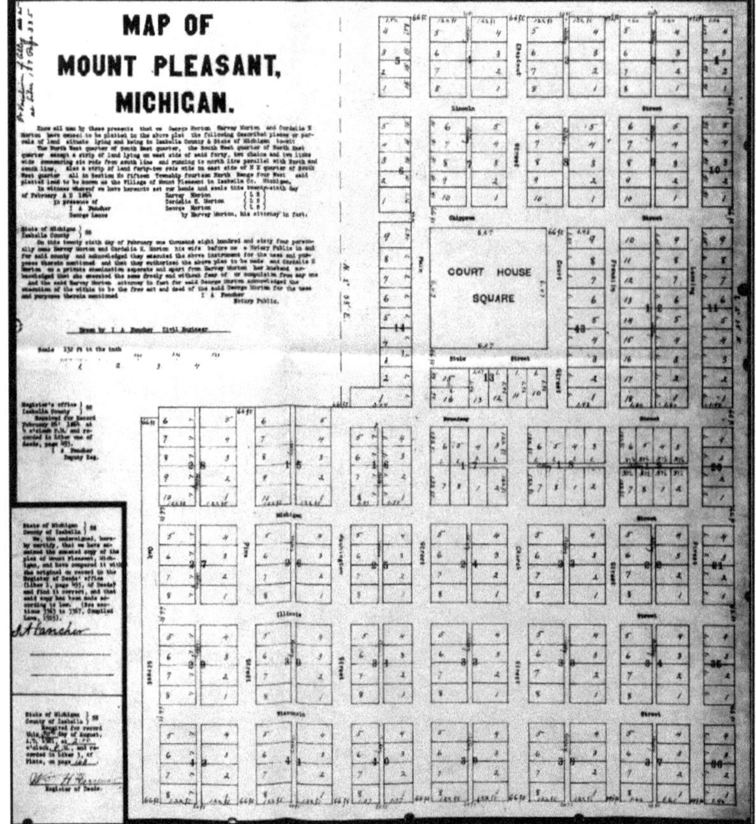

1864 Plat of Mt. Pleasant

In 1860, the first rough plat of the settlement of Mt. Pleasant was made by David Ward, laying out the village on his recently timbered 200 acres on the bluff overlooking the east bank of the Chippewa River's "S" turn of its route from upper Isabella County origins to juncture with the Tittabawassee River at Midland. Ward sold the platted settlement to the Morton Brothers of New York and offered the newly-formed Isabella County five acres for their county building if the county seat moved from Isabella City, a.k.a. Indian Mills, to the newly platted land. In 1863, when civil engineer Isaac A. Fancher and his wife Althea Preston Fancher moved to Mt. Pleasant, and bought three lots in the 300 block of North Main Street. Fancher, ever the perfectionist, was not content with Ward's crude plat and surveyed the plat, submitting this revised version to the State of Michigan in February 1864. The plat was accepted and 21 years later, Mt. Pleasants government was officially recognized with organization as a village in 1885,

Special Dedication

To Samuel W. Hopkins: Primary reason most of our homes are here

"The commodious, modern and attractive home of Mr. and Mrs. Hopkins is a park-like place, the wide, spacious lawns being shady and inviting, ornamental and fruit trees, shrubbery, vines and flowers being in profusion, and because ten stately oaks grow near this beautiful residence the place is known as Oakten. It is on Normal Avenue and in the most desirable residence portion of the city. Here the many friends of the family often gather, finding an old-time hospitality and good cheer ever prevailing. The house is equipped with a splendid and carefully selected library, where Mr. Hopkins spends many pleasant hours, losing himself "in other men's minds," and is familiar with the world's best literature."

Isaac A. Fancher
Past and Present of Isabella County
1911

The above word picture of the home of Samuel Whalen and Margaretta Hopkins home was part of Fancher's nine page tribute to Hopkins in his book. The house was located at **630 South Normal Street, now University Avenue**, unfortunately, the best we can do to represent the man who probably is the single biggest factor in conversion from this sleepy lumber town in the middle of a swamp on a bluff overlooking the Chippewa River to a thriving manufacturing and educational center leading up to the dawn of the 20th Century. The last remnants of the house described, burned in an August, 1974 fire, 51 years after Hopkins 1923 death.

While no single individual can build a town and make it grow, the vision, ambition and leadership of Samuel W. Hopkins, left *in 1884*, was responsible for practically every major milestone in Mt. Pleasants commercial and educational history until the early 1920s.

It is appropriate the official re-

At September 18, 1892, ceremonies the Central Michigan Normal School and Business Institute, officially broke ground for the school's first building on a ten acre plot south of town. On November 19, 1892, the cornerstone of the first building was laid in ceremonies conducted by the Knights of Pythias.

lease date of this book should be five days after the 120th Anniversary of the laying of the cornerstone of the first building on the original Central campus at Mt. Pleasant. But more about that later.

Samuel W. Hopkins was born in April 1845, in Exeter, Rhode Island, the youngest of eight children of Judge Samuel and Freelove Burlingame Arnold Hopkins. He was a descendant of Declaration of Independence signer Stephen Hopkins. Learning came easy to Samuel W. and by age three he knew by heart Young's *First Reader* and Webster's *Spelling Book*, the two books he possessed. By eleven he could read and write, and by fourteen, with an invalid mother, two invalid sisters and a father with broken health, he was pretty much on his own while helping the others and striving for a higher education. In 1865, he graduated Fenton and Bigelow College in Cleveland, Ohio and began reading law with Benzeret H. Bill of Rockville, Ohio. In the fall of 1870, he entered the law department of the University of Michigan, graduating there in 1872, after which he visited his old home for awhile before returning to Michigan to locate in Grand Rapids, where he was admitted to the bar and did estate work that put him in central and northern Michigan.

While in Clare, he met Mt. Pleasant attorney/surveyor/businessman Isaac A. Fancher, who convinced him to come to Isabella County and join Fancher's legal practice. They were partners for three years. Hopkins then partnered with Michael Devereaux and Wade Smith for two years before partnering with a law school friend Free Estee. Hopkins was appointed Isabella County Clerk in 1873 and was then elected to three terms. He was justice of the peace for seven years. In 1874, he platted the Hopkins Addition to the City of Mt. Pleasant. He also served as Isabella

County Prosecuting Attorney in 1875-76, then was elected to the Michigan Legislature in 1876 and re-elected in 1879, serving four years.

1892 was a busy year for Mr. Hopkins, he was elected to the Michigan Senate, he was chairman of the Mt. Pleasant Businessman's Association in charge of working to locate the United States Indian Industrial School in Isabella County. His correspondence with the area's district Congressman Bliss, secured the location for Mt. Pleasant.

That same year, he conceived of the idea of platting land and selling it to apply the proceeds to erecting a normal school here.

According to the Wikipedia online dictionary –"A **normal school** was a school created to train high school graduates to be teachers. Its purpose was to establish teaching standards or *norms*, hence its name. Most such schools are now called **teachers' colleges**; however, in some places, the term *normal school* is still used."

In the late 1800s, the teachers of Isabella County each year held a Teachers Institute at the county seat in Mt. Pleasant. During these institutes, tests would be given to high school graduates who wanted to become school teachers. If the person passed the tests, they were awarded a Teacher's Certificate. The number of one-room rural schools in the county , *ultimately to reach 115,* was growing and the demand for teachers was intense. Yet in 1882, the week-long summer institute was sparsely attended.

By 1890, there were an estimated 4,500 students regularly attending classes an average seven months per year, according to *The Enterprise* newspaper. These students were taught by 136 teachers, of which only three had teacher's certificates.

By 1892, the month-long summer normal had only 45 enrollees. The final test failure rate was so high that it was determined that the establishment of a formal normal school was needed. The year before only 10 out of 58 passed the teachers test.

M. K. Skinner, who had bought H. W. Jordan's Pen Art and Business College in 1891 planned to make improvements and add a full normal course, so people who wish to be teachers could earn a teachers certificate.

Samuel Hopkins, knowing 60 acres of the old Hursh farm at the south city limits were available, sketched a proposed sub-division, believing the sale of lots would make enough money to finance erection of a normal school building. He approached others with his plan.

Hopkins talked it over with friend, farmer and fellow member of the board of education Charles Brooks, who reacted favorably. The two shared the idea with John W. Hance, Michael Devereaux and A. S. Cotant. That five then invited Wilkinson Doughty, George Dusenbury, Isaac A. Fancher, M. Lower, Douglas Nelson, F. D. Patterson, and L. N. Smith, to serve on a planning committee with them. The twelve formed the Mount Pleasant Improvement Company with a capital of $10,000 in shares of $25, which bought the 60 Hursh acres. Eight acres had already been subdivided, so company land consisted of 52 acres, with ten acres set aside for the college campus. The company sold 151 housing lots at a July 4, 1892, auction, for $110 each with the buyer asked to place $10 down and pay $10 per month for the second and third months and $5 per month on the balance until paid.

On September 13, 1892, the Central Michigan Normal School and Business Institute opened its doors on the second floor of the Carpenter Building at the southeast corner of Main and Michigan Streets. The building burned in the late 1990s. Five days later, the cornerstone was laid for the first building on the campus of what is now Central Michigan University.

Samuel W. Hopkins, *left in 1910*, later was President of the Mt. Pleasant Sugar Company and succeeded after years of effort to get the Michigan Condensed Milk Company to locate a plant in Mt. Pleasant at 300 West Broadway, later the Borden building, now Mt. Pleasant City Hall. Additionally, he was responsible for bringing achicory processing plant to Mt. Pleasant.

Samuel and Margaretta Hopkins were married in 1873 had one son who died at one year old, and a daughter Lila Vedder, who married and moved to Gaylord, Michigan, then Detroit, with husband Jay Harris Buell.

While a member of the School Board, Hopkins took an active part in locating three sites for schools and erecting five school buildings. He worked with and made liberal contributions to the erection of the Isabella County Courthouse, the railroads, and the establishment of a Dow Chemical salt works at the north edge of Mt. Pleasant.

Margaretta Hopkins died in 1919 and Samuel W. Hopkins followed in 1923, having kept the towns commerce in steady growth and prepared for the oil boom that followed the discovery of the Mt. Pleasant oilfield in 1928, spurring the town's growth to new heights. Hopkins would have rejoiced.

Curiously, only a short street named after him is Mt. Pleasants sole tribute to Samuel W. Hopkins, scant reminder of the godfather of its growth.

North End
(North of Broadway to Pickard)

North:
Arnold, Court, Fancher, Franklin, Kinney, Lansing, Main, Mission, University (Church, Normal, College), and Washington Streets

202 (right) and 210 North Arnold are identical twin floor plan houses built in the gable front and wing family style of architecture descended from the Greek Revival style used often in rural areas. The houses were built in 1894, probably on speculation by John Kinney. It was popular for developers to plat additions and build houses for sale after addition to the town. In 1926, the homes were occupied by Hugh G. Johnson (202) and Perle Wilcox (210) with his wife Minnie. Both Johnson and Wilcox were employees of Gorham Brothers, manufacturers of truck slats and veneers. Later, 202 was owned by E. C. Utterback family while 210 stayed in the Wilcox family until the early 1960s.

209 North Arnold was built in 1936 by C. Dale and his wife Ilma Richmond. Richmond was a hardware merchant and principal in Richmond Shangle Hardware at 121 South Main Street in Mt. Pleasant.

Later owner/occupants included Central Michigan University Professor Lynn Baird Tipson, his wife Sarah and son David in 1963 and Sam and Gertrude Staples in 1987.

Between Arnold and North Mission in the alley behind the 500 and 600 blocks of North Arnold a curious plethora of "apparent garage and shed converted to small house" structures exist, some still occupied. All seem to have been converted in the late 1920s and early 1930s, possibly because of the housing crunch brought about by the oil boom prompted by the 1928 Mt. Pleasant Field discovery which meant work during the Great Depression while other parts of the country suffered. Normally these alley adjacent residences are seen on the south end of town, closer to Central Michigan University. The proximity to then U.S. 27 (Mission Street) may also have been a factor. Besides 608½ North Arnold and 521 ½ North Arnold the small house brigade between North Arnold and North Mission in the 500s and 600s includes houses shown below.

516½ North Arnold, below, and 612 ½ North Arnold, above.

501 and 503 North Arnold Here is another pair of what the author has chosen to dub "architectural cousins". While the main body of the houses design is similar, with a deeper pitch to the roof of the house on the left, the mirror-imaged gabled front entries, a kinship in builder or designer, probably because of the same last names of the builders.

501 North Arnold, left Apparently Mt. Pleasant Water Department's Wynan Paullin liked the looks of the house next door so well that in 1935 he built one almost like it for he and his wife Bernadine, a clerk at Exchange Savings Bank. In the 1960s, the Paullins sold the house to Francis E. Eisman in 1972. In 2002, Victor and Virgie Eisman, sold the house to John and Nancy Theisen. The Theisens sold the homes to Albana Amanda Lulguraj, who sold it in 2012 to Scott Kinsey.

503 North Arnold, right, was the first built, in 1932, by Kenneth Paullin, a clerk, who later became the owner of Ken's Mens Shop at 109 East Broadway. In 1958, the house was sold to Martha Claus, owner of the M & M Bar at 110 West Michigan, who in 1993 turned it over to son Maurice Claus.

619 North Arnold was born in 1894, according to City of Mt. Pleasant Tax Assessing Service records and spent the first 68 years of its life over on North Mission Street.

In 1962, *above*, the house was moved to it's present address by Kinney School Principal Harley Hinkley and his wife Brigid, a Registered Nurse with Central Michigan Health Services. Together they raised daughters Anne, Beth, Christa, Dina and Elaine. The growing Hinkley family required ever-increasing space, so the house was expanded and remodeled several times, *below in 2012 with the front facing unchange in style*,.

Leo R. and Marilyn G. Wickert bought the home in 1978 and in 2002, the Wickerts sold the house to Gary and Vicki Green.

700-708 North Arnold are shown as backdrop to these mid-1950s Kinney School kids playing ball at recess. Looking east at the 700 block of North Arnold Street, right to left:

700 – C. M. Merrifield, a truck driver, and his wife Lillian as well as Ernest W. Merrifield, also a truck driver.

702 – Chris Nolan, a trucker, and his wife Irene along with children Wayne, Joan, Adverna, Sara Sue and Lorna Lee. Also Harold Reynolds, a truck driver and his wife Betty.

704 - James Freeze. Freeze had a small "front room" grocery in his home, from which he sold penny candy. Kinney school kids were forbidden to cross the dirt road that was Arnold Street during recess. So of course Freeze's candy counter was a mad-house during Kinney recess.

706 – Archie Leonard, a trucker, and his wife Markeith.

708 - Leon Burr, a trucker, and his wife Gladys, along with children Leon Jr., Erma, Kenneth and Charles.

A decade later, the 700 block of North Arnold Street was vacated to expand the Kinney School playground to the alley behind businesses in the 700 block of North Mission and the entire complex was later fenced.

202-204 North Court Street Mt. Pleasant's early medical care needs were served by doctor's offices in the doctor's homes or small offices in downtown buildings. Doctor Michael F. Brondstetter, *far left in above photo*, purchased the house in the center at 202 Court Street from Dr. J. Franklin Adams and converted it to a hospital in 1915. Dr. Brondstetter died in February, 1931, at age 46, and the hospital was sold to Dr. L. F. Hyslop in 1932. Later, the Dr. McArthur- Dr. Strange partnership built a two story building just north of the Brondstetter hospital building, replacing the house at the left in the top picture.

Built in 1936, the new McArthur-Strange Hospital at **204 Court**, *right,* was two stories high, adjacent to the Brondstetter Hospital at **202 Court.** Known as the Wood Building, the new structure was used for doctor's offices, storage and labs for the original Brondstetter Hospital.

202 Court was razed to accommodate, the push-through of Mosher Street to Main in the 1970s. In 2012, *below,* the Wood building is occupied in the southwest corner by Tom and Donna Murphy as a residence, with the rest of the building occupied by the offices of Always Me Bail Bonds; Cindy Kaliszewski CPA and Jostens.

213 and 315 North Fancher A tale of two brothers and two Cape Cod-style homes on North Fancher Street. Oil and gas drilling contractor Noah F. Andrew and his wife Lola built the first of the pair in 1932 at 213 North Fancher, *above.* Apparently Noah's brother Earl Andrews, also of Union Rotary Drilling, like the Cape Cod style and the North Fancher neighborhood so well that in 1937 he and wife Lena bought 315 North Fancher, which was on the property owned by Charles Wildemuth at 315 East Chippewa and had been the carriage house for that residence. In 1940, Noah rented 213 to oilfield service contractor William Donaldson and his wife Margaret, who later moved. In 1963, the Andrews sold 213 to attorney Edward N. Lynch and his wife Dorothy. In 1978, the home sold to Robert S, Mellott and his wife Karen. Since 2002, it has belonged to Jeffrey and Carol Ellis Co-Trust.

Meanwhile, in the 1960s, the widowed Lola Andrews sold 315 North Fancher to Robert Heintz, Senior and his wife Margaret "Tat" Heintz.

219 North Fancher is a "Stick" style Victorian home typical of the kind built 1882 by Mt. Pleasant pioneer hardware dealer Levi N. Smith and his wife Eva, shortly after their wedding at Hudson, Michigan. When Levi Smith arrived in Mt. Pleasant in 1872, there were only 40 buildings in the town. He had learned the tinners trade in his native Lenawee County and set up a hardware store, renting the east half of Isaac A. Fancher's block at the northeast corner of Broadway and Main, built of brick after the original burned in the great fire of 1875. In 1894, Smith built his own building at 121 South Main. The Smiths owned the home until 1906, when they sold it to Gustur and Julia Tonnett and moved to Beulah. Levi N. Smith died in 1908.

In 1925, the house was sold to William and Sabina Carroll, a building contractor, who sold it in 1930, to Charles Stewart Harkins and his wife Jane. Harkins worked for Harris Milling Company and was later a mechanic for Ford garages in Shepherd and Mt. Pleasant. Jane Harkins was a teacher. Together they raised son Richard and daughter Beatrice. In 1939, the Harkins sold to Mt. Pleasant Hardware employee Cloice Hileman and his wife Nellie, a clerk at Gover City & Discount Store. Part of the house, a small apartment on the south side, became a rental occupied for a time by George Hileman and his wife Blanche, oil worker Charles Brown, painter Albert E. Fraser and Ray Ryzenga and CMU student Susan Franen through the years.

In 1972, the house was sold to James R. Rush and in 1975 to Benson and Janet Chiesa.

222 North Fancher The original home was built in 1891 by Arwin E. Gorham, below right, Vice President of Gorham Brothers Co., Mt. Pleasant's largest and most prestigious lumber company and saw mill. Arwin E. Gorham built a huge home at the corner of Fancher and Chippewa Streets, angled to face both and neither. Gorham came to Mt. Pleasant when the company moved its business interests here in 1888. A. E. Gorham married Sarah M. Balmer of Mt. Pleasant in 1891. He was connected with the Exchange Savings Bank, becoming its President in 1905. Mr. Gorham died in 1931.

In 1935, oil producer Edward Stewart and his wife Mollie bought the property and leveled the house, using the foundation as the basis for a brick Cape Cod-style home, enshrouded in trees and exquisite landscaping in 2012, *below*. Here they raised sons David, J. Russell, Norman, John and William. In 1969, the house was sold to dentist William R. Fortino and his wife Ruth, who raised daughters Mia Jane, Anne M., and Kristy, along with sons William, Michael, Brian, and Jon here. In 1991, the house was sold to landscaper Gary Sova and his wife Vicki..

317 North Fancher was built in 1890 by Isabella County *Enterprise* newspaper owner Arthur Stanley Coutant, *right*, and his wife Anna. In 1892, Coutant was one of twelve Mt. Pleasant citizens who organized the Central Normal School. In 1918, the Coutants sold to John Conley, who sold in 1922 to Assistant Exchange Bank cashier Walter S. Horn and his wife Bernice. In 1934, Horn sold the house to Atlas Supply's James S. Leggett and his wife Agnes, who sold to geologist William A.Thomas and his wife Jessie, who in turn sold in 1945 to oilman Edward Prior, Jr. and his wife Imogene.

The Michigan oil and gas exploration and production connection to the address continued when in 1957, the Priors sold to oilman Kavanaugh P. (K.P.) Wood, Jr., *left*, and his wife Eleanor (Russell). K. P., with partner Thomas Mask, was co-discoverer of the Scipio extension of the Albion-Scipio oilfield, Michigan's only field to have produced more than 100 million barrels of oil from a contiguous reservoir. In 1965, the Woods sold to retiree Thomas Pell and his wife Julia. Thomas Pell died in 1978 and Julia followed in 2009. In 2010, the Pell estate sold the house to Keith and Kimberly Cotter.

325 North Fancher, above in 1906 Lumberman Franklin and his wife Faithful Whitehead built the core of the house in 1885 and added the large wraparound porch around 1900. The house was best known as the Edgar A.(Ed.) Bixby, of Mt. Pleasant Hardware, house. In the 1960s, it was the home of City Mt. Pleasant Director of Public Safety H. E. Haun and his wife Vivian. Dwight and Betty Reava bought the home in the 1970s and lived there in 1992, when it was included on the Mt. Pleasant Area Historical Society Christmas House Walk. The dining room rugs then were original to the house, but had traveled to a farm house and then to Lansing for a time until retrieved by the Reavas in the 1980's.

In the 1990s the house was a bed and breakfast inn until returning to private residency. During his tenure as Central Michigan University Assistant Football Coach, "Butch" Jones and family were residents. The house, left, belongs to Frank and Mary Beth Rowland in 2012.

326 North Fancher has been occupied by only two families since construction and was named a Centennial Home and was a Mt. Pleasant Area Historical Society Christmas Walk Home in 1989.

The home was built in 1890 by early Mt. Pleasant clothier William. E. Lewis, *below*, who married John Kinney's daughter Bertha that same year. Lewis was born in Fremont, Ohio, in 1863 and came to Mt. Pleasant in 1881. Lewis partnered with Louis N. Marsh *(see 401 South Fancher)* in 1889 to form Marsh and Lewis clothiers at the southeast corner of Broadway and Main streets, site of John Kinney's first log cabin/general store. John Kinney died in this house in 1919.

Later, Lewis dissolved the partnership to form W. E. Lewis & Sons, a clothing store located at 117 East Broadway, later to become Beatty & White Men's Shop, then the Gentry men's clothing store and, in 2012, Jimmy John's Sandwich Shop. The 1926 Mt. Pleasant City Directory notes that Mr. Lewis "drove a Buick".

Lewis later turned the business over to his son, C. Kinney Lewis, who died in November, 1938. His wife continued the business.

The senior Lewis was a founding member of the Mt. Pleasant Rotary Club. He was also elected to the Mt. Pleasant City Commission and in 1931 helped formulate the city charter that established the city-manager system, a form of government not used by many municipalities.

Lewis was President of the Exchange Bank 1929-1935, at the location of his first clothing store, later serving on the bank's board of directors. He was a member of the Mt. Pleasant Board of Education for 11 years, during the school system's expansion.

William E. Lewis died at home in March, 1939.

The house remained in the Lewis family until 1944 , then purchased by the late Clifford W. and Dorothy Collin of the oilfield service company Evaluation Sales & Service, 211 East Pickard. Their offspring included: C. W. "Bill", Jim, Susan, David L., Jon, Dennis, Marie, Catherine, Gene, and Paul Collin.

Cliff Collin, *right*, who raised the house and added a basement, later became an independent petroleum explorer/producer, who flew his own airplane to supervise drilling of his wells, a practice that proved fatal in November 11, 1968.

Among many wells Collin drilled statewide, his most locally famous was his Albar 1, drilled with Frank Rand in the summer of 1950 just west of Mt. Pleasant in Section 20 of Union Township. The discovery of oil there caused a leasing boom but proved to be a one well field. All told, the one well Union 20 Field produced 58,263 barrels of oil and 55.05 million cubic feet of natural gas before 1963 abandonment. Four dry offsets surround the site of Albar 1 on oilfield maps today and a communication antenna tower marks the spot where Collin's rig once was the center of joy and speculation. A 2012 well drilled in the area was a dry hole

In the 1970s, the house was occupied by Cliff's daughter Susan and her husband Don R. Fuller (*see 312 North Franklin). When the Fullers moved two blocks west, Jon Collin moved in with his family in 1978.

401 North Fancher The house was built in 1894 by Anson R. Arnold and sold in 1905 to Mrs. A. F. Vandercook. In 1914 the house and property was acquired by Daniel Buckley, *see 409 North Fancher*, who sold in 1919 to Ernest R. Dexter. Dexter came to Mt. Pleasant in 1911 from his native Saginaw County, where he had served as supervisor of his township until appointed Deputy Clerk of the Saginaw County Road Commission for two terms. Dexter came to town with his brother-in-law, John P. McCall, brother of his first wife Leota. Leota died before Dexter's arrival here. Together they ran McCall and Dexter Implement Store, buying the stock and business of Ed Smithers on West Broadway. The farm implement and harness business operated until 1935. Meantime, Dexter married the former Mabel Neff in 1933.

In 1918, Ernest Dexter was elected Treasurer for the City of Mt. Pleasant, a position he held until 1923, when he resigned to run for State Representative for Isabella County, winning the seat in which he served for six years. During that term, he also served as secretary of the Isabella County Poor Commission for ten years. In 1930, he was elected Isabella County Clerk and served until 1935, when he retired. Dexter died in 1958 and his wife lived in the house until her 1972 death. The Mabel Dexter estate sold to Archey Sporting Goods Manager Robert A. Archey Jr. and his wife Susan A. in 1972. Here the Archeys raised Bobby, Jennifer and Ryan.

Mt. Pleasant attorney Gordon Bloem and his wife Nancy J. Parshall purchased the house in 1997.

404 North Fancher Built by J. E. Chatterton & Sons Elevator Manager Howard E. Chatteron in 1919. This tile roofed Prairie style brick home is an extension of the bungalow design in a number of ways but more expensive to build. It is greater in size and expanded out in long horizontal wings, requiring a larger lot, which the northeast corner of Fancher and Lincoln streets supplies.

The northwest corner of Main and Lincoln, has always been a busy corner as the Horning Grain Elevator did business at the corner, alongside the entrance to what is now Island Park, until 1903 when J. E. and son Howard E. Chatterton left the grocery business and bought the mill, renaming it J. E. Chatterton & Son.

In 1928, the house was owned by Glen G. Knapp, manager of Mt. Pleasant Produce at 401 North Main Street in Mt. Pleasant. The house was owned twice by auto dealer J. F. Battle first for several years in the 1930s, then selling to Leonard Pipeline owner David E. Beach in the 1940s and taking it back from a land contract in the 1950s. An eight page supplement to the *Isabella County Times* announced the opening of the J. F. Battle ultra-modern automobile dealership at 702 East Broadway April 7, 1938. Battle continued business until the 1950s, when C. Floyd Smale bought the Chevrolet Dealership. Later it became Archey Brothers Sales and Service until the 1990s when the building became the business home of Murray Wholesale, operating from there in 2010.

After Battle, the house was home to Hilliard Drilling Company William "Billy" Hilliard and his wife Edna. from 1958 until 1979. when house was purchased by Earl and Sharon Hartman, who have continually maintained the historic and architectural integrity of the house.

409 North Fancher The house was built in 1894 by Anson Arnold. In 1914, the house was purchased probably by one of the most colorful personalities to live on North Fancher, and maybe in Mt. Pleasant.

Military veteran and retired farmer Daniel Buckley was 69 years old when his 27 year old second wife and their five year old son Herman R. Buckley moved into this house.

The saga of Daniel Buckley is so fascinating that Isaac A. Fancher devoted one and a third pages to him in Fancher's 1911 local historians "Bible" Isabella County: Past and Present and the *Isabella County Times* newspaper devoted almost a foot of news type to his passing in 1952.

Daniel Buckley's life story reads like an adventure novel.

Born in 1845 in Norfolk County, Ontario, Canada, Buckley lost his mother to death in 1853 and was bound out as a tailor's apprentice. He liked neither the trade or his master and wasn't impressed with the idea of so long a tenure of service, so he took off as soon as an opportunity arose and made his way to Detroit, Michigan. In Detroit he signed on with a crew to drive horses to St. Louis, Missouri, which put even more distance between him and the abandoned Canadian apprenticeship. When he was paid for the St. Louis drive, he took his pay and went to Nashville, Tennessee, where he was hired by the United States Government as a teamster, but resigned after three months to return to his home province to spend the following year at home.

At 20 years old, in 1865 he returned to Detroit where he enlisted in Nineteenth United States Infantry Company A 37th Regiment, later he was assigned to Company K, Third Infantry as a corporal.

During his six years in the Army, he fought frontier battles, did garrison duty at Western outposts, carried dispatches and drove stagecoach between Fort Wingate, Santa Fe, and Albuquerque. Trinidad and other New Mexico out posts. He also was a scout and part of the famous Seventh Cavalry, under the command of General Custer, during Custer's first trip to the plains. Buckley left the Army at the end of his six year enlistment, in 1872 (missing Custer's Battle of Little Bighorn by six years). He returned to Ontario for a year before deciding to come to Isabella County, Michigan, to help his brother Tom operate a store in Isabella City.

Buckley worked at several lumber camps here before purchasing 40 acres in Section 36 of Isabella County, which he cleared and converted to cultivation to make it one of the finest farms in the county.

His first marriage to wife, Marie Annis, bore four children - Harry, Ray, Thomas and Kate. Marie Annis died in 1905 and in 1907, Dan Buckley married 20 year old Nancy "Nan" Ann McClain.

Left to right in this 1920s photo are: Nancy Ann McClain-Buckley, Dan Buckley, his son Herman and his daughter by his first wife, Kate Buckley-Wombacker.

Daniel Buckley died in 1933 and, according to the newspaper account of his death "In honor to the great soldier that Mr. Buckley was as well as an esteemed pioneer and citizen, the local post of the American Legion will march in a body for the services."

Nan Buckley, an active participant in the Women's Relief Corps, a woman's auxiliary to the Grand Army of the Republic and later American Legion, died in 1965.

The home's next owner was son Herman R. Buckley, a 20 year truck driver for Valley Chemical Company of Mt. Pleasant and his wife Blanche, *left with baby daughter Marlene.* Here the Buckley's raised six sons - Daniel, Gerald, Richard, James, Thomas and William, as well as four daughters – Helen Marlene, Shirley, Nancy and Sharon. Herman Buckley died in 1993 and Blanche followed in 2008.

Later owners of the house included: Lenora Forist and Karen Green; Virginia K. Rousseau; and, since 2006 James & Kylee Johnson.

501 North Fancher Base structure is on an 1884 bird's eye view line drawing of Mt. Pleasant and probably was built that year by Frederick Nebling,. Occupants of the house have included insurance agent Hugh Watson and his wife Edith 1920 to mid 1930s and Frigidaire Service Technician for Consumers Power, Edward F. McKenna and his wife Margaret in the 1930s. Spang Oilfield Supply Company Office Manager Charles McCamnet and his wife Gertrude bought the place in the 1940s and raised daughters Wilma and Martha there. Heating and cooling technician Keith Gothup and his wife Mary Veronica owned the home from the late 1950s and raised children James, Janet and Jill here.

In 1968, the house was bought by future Michigan Oil & Gas News magazine managing Editor Jack R. Westbrook and his wife Mary Lou, a financial advertising copywriter. They raised Lydia, Collette, Steve, Paula and Mary here. The rendering of the house in watercolors, reproduced in black and white *right*, was done by Paula now Westbrook-Parrish of Garden Grove, California, in 1985 when the house was just 100 years old. The house was designated a Centennial Home in 1989.

506 North Fancher, "the big yellow brick house with the lions", has long boasted stone lions flanking the front porch steps and for a time in the 1990s, above, the back porch steps. The house was built of distinctive pale yellow "Mt. Pleasant brick" in 1900 by dry goods merchant Albert W. Graham and his wife Caroline. The A. W. Graham Dry Goods and Floor Covering store was at 122 East Broadway. Albert Graham died in 1927 and Caroline continued to live there until her 1949 death. The home became a rental property and converted to a two flat structure in 1940. For a time following his wife's death, grocery store/meat marketer Louis DuHamel, whose store was at the northwest corner of Fancher and Andre Streets, rented the upstairs apartment with his son Bill. From 1949 until 1968, the house was home to John F. Battle and his wife Bernice. In 1958, the house was purchased by Edward A. VanDyne of VanDyne Hardware, 121 South Main Street, and the apartment was rented to Mae N. Walker, an employee of Dowell oilfield service company. During the 1960s, the address was home to oilfield drilling superintendent Gyle Atterburry and his wife Irene. Purchased by the late CMU Counselor James Owen in 1970, who died in 1991. It was renovated in the 1980s by travel agent Maryanke Owen, who lived there from 1981 until 1995, closed off the apartment, returning the home to single-family occupancy, as it remains. She installed an open stairway and oak mantle, an antique hall tree from England, and a 1947 metal carousel horse for display at the entrance. The front rooms were offices for Maryanke Travel into the 1990s. Maryanke occupied the building in 1992, when the home was included on the Mt. Pleasant Area Historical Society Christmas House Walk. John and Sue Bleik bought the home. In 1995, Bleik was the first manager of the hotel segment of the Saginaw Chippewa Indian Tribe's Soaring Eagle Resort and supervised much of the hotel's design while it was being constructed. Most recent owners are Ken and Betty Blevins.

522 North Fancher The house was built in 1900 when Anna Marsh owned the property. Beginning in the 1930s, the address was home to Claud and Margaret Whitcomb and part of the house was given over to renters. Following Calud's death, Margaret maintained offices for the American Red Cross in her home, *above in 1981*, for many years until failing health caused her to pass the Red Cross responsibilities to (Mrs. George) Frances Heynig next door at 518 North Fancher. The same ill health led to the sale of the home in 1984 to Gerald and Margaret Travis , who recently installed new siding, *below*.

606 North Fancher Avenue and 509 East Andre Both properties are listed under the ownership of the Harvey and Emeline Francisco in 1899, when 606 North Fancher, *above*, was built. Emeline survived Harvey by many years, succumbing in 1930, at which time the property was sold to Garrett Filmore VanWie and his wife. Clarissa. At this time, it is believed that, prompted by Mt. Pleasant's oil boom, the 509 Andre house, *below,* was built and is listed as a subaddress to the North Fancher house in official records. Garrett VanWie died in 1935 and Clarissa in 1962, at which time the house was sold to Hood Lumber Company's (115 West Pickard) President Robert Hood and his wife Helen, a Beal City teacher. By the 1970s, succeeding owners turned the house into a rental property. The little house on the alley, 509 Andre, has been home to Roosevelt Refinery's John Metheany and his wife Virginia; Mrs. William Garvin; Consumers Power bookeepers Misses Rose and Mary Carroll; Ferro Manufacturing company machinist John Stevens; J. Casteel and others since the 1980s.

721 North Fancher is enclosed by trees and a picket fence and so is difficult to photograph but is included in this volume for a very special reason. At a December, 2010, book signing, Sher Muszynski asked me "What can you tell me about my house?" I said. "Nothing, but I'll look it up and tell you." That research put the author on the path that led to this book.

The house was built in 1904 by Theodore Perry and his wife Dora, who sold in 1946 to Austin Furnace and Heating owner Leroy M. Austin and his wife Ella A. Here the Austins raised William, Donna J. and Margie K.

In 1963, the Austins sold the house to Dow Chemical's Wallace Eugene and Esther Jean Morey. Here the Morey's lived with children Pamela, Jackalynn, Cynthia, Kimberly and David. Wallace Morey died in 1964 and Jean lived here with the children until 1974, when she sold to Mt. Pleasant school system teacher Sher Musyzynski, *right,* who started at the elementary school level, then spent 30 years at the junior high level teaching visual arts and art history, retiring in 2010. Sher died suddenly June 21, 2012, on the eve of a trip to Italy with her husband dentist Dr. Daniel Kane.

The author joins the family in wishing Sher could be here to see this book and know what her question prompted.

311 North Franklin, above in the 1970s, was built in the early 1890s by pharmacist P. Cory Taylor, whose drug store at 124 South Main also sold wallpaper. In 1897, Taylor sold the place to Edward C. Smithers and his wife Teresa, who, after Edward's 1931 death lived there until she died in 1939. Their daughter Teresa G. Smithers, a teacher, died there in 1956 and the estate sold the home to Malcomb McShea of Taylor Oil Company. McShea was Mt. Pleasant's Mayor in 1948. In 1970, the house was bought by Wayne E. Van Dyke, a Mt. Pleasant policeman, and his practical nurse wife Mary, who would raise children Phillip, Mark, Kathy, Becky, Loretta, and David. The Van Dykes, now detective and Nurses Training specialist at Mt. Pleasant High School respective, sold to Chris and Rebecca Bundy in 1992. The Bundys massively remodeled the home in the mid-1990s, below.

312 North Franklin, above in 2012, oral history says was built in 1864 as a carriage house for the Wilkinson P. Doughty residence, *see 301 East Chippewa.* Wilkinson Doughty, along with brother Jared Doughty, *see 202 South University*, were leading pioneer merchants in the fledgling village of Mt. Pleasant. The structure was moved forward and converted to a residence in 1922 according to City of Mt. Pleasant Assessing records. The carriage house area is now the living room and the present dining room occupies space that was once the stables, while the upstairs was sometimes used as a children's theater.

From 1922 until 1958, the house was occupied by a renter, car salesman W.W. Seger and his wife Olivia. In 1958, machinist Harold N. Chamberlain lived there, followed by custodian of the First Methodist Church Robert E. Miller and his wife Helen, a housekeeper. In 1972, the house was occupied by Mt. Pleasant State Home and Training School Physician Kanil S. Cankir and his wife Gulgen. By 1978, Mary S. Duffy an employee of the Mt. Pleasant Center for Human Development, as well as Muriel Kniffen and Jan Russell lived there.

In 1978, the house was purchased by Donald "Roger" Fuller and his wife Susan (Collin) Fuller, who owned the property when it was included in the 1993 Mt. Pleasant Area Historical Society's Annual Christmas House Walk. The house was one of those honored as a Centennial Home during the City of Mt. Pleasant's 1989 celebration of the 100th Anniversary of the town's charter as a city.

323 North Franklin left This home was built in 1894 by Jay and Anna Crittenton and sold to John and Mary Bailey in 1922, who sold to carpenter Charles Hibbeln in 1933, then interior decorator Clinton L. Comins and his wife Lena bought the house in 1939 and lived here until Clinton's 1955 death. Here they raised James, Bessie, Mary and Jane Ann. Here, also for a period in the 1940s and early 1950s, they ran Comins Maternity Home. Since 1955, there have been 10 transactions regarding this home, concluding with ownership under the Alberta McBride Trust.

401 North Franklin also known as 215 East Lincoln right Built in 1838 by Charles Hibbeln, the house was purchased by Standard Oil bulk distributor Lorne Coyne and his wife Elsie in the early 1940s. Here they raised son Daniel G., named for Lorne's father. In 1963, when Dan and wife Melva moved family and the business, which he now operated, to this address and as they did on Lansing street, created an address on the Lincoln Street side of the house so that customers of the bulk oil business would come to that door instead of the residence door facing Lincoln Street. Here Dan G. and Melva raised sons David, Dana and Mark, who was born in 1956 and celebrated his 56th birthday while this book was being written. Meantime, Lorne and Elsie moved down the street to ***401 East Lincoln, left***. Elsie died in 1970 and Lorne followed in 1978, after maintaining a meticulous lawn at his last home for years.

205 North Kinney, above in 2012, as depicted in pastels by Mt. Pleasant artist David Ellis This Spanish Colonial Revival style home was built in the late 1920s by Mt. Pleasant's American Enamel Products, founder August J. Smith and his wife Marie. American Enamel Company was a manufacturing company alongside the railroad tracks on the south side of west Pickard, in the business center that was built as Transport Trucks in the 1920s, morphed into Ferro Stamping Company in the 1940s and now houses the offices of Mt. Pleasant's daily newspaper, *The Morning Sun*.

Originally from New Jersey, Smith was raised in the east, then went to Chicago, where he was involved in manufacturing for a number of years before coming to Mt. Pleasant and founding American Enamel in 1926. It is said that Smith designed this home himself and that the original blueprints of the home still reside there with the current owner. August Smith died in 1936 at 68 years old, shortly after his dream home was completed, leaving his wife, a son Edwin and a daughter Grace. Marie followed him at 80 years old in 1967, at the *3605 Grawn Avenue*, Mt. Pleasant home of her niece, Mrs. Donald Carr, having survived both her son and daughter.

In the late 1930s, Marie Smith had sold the home to real estate man Charles J. Myers and his wife Marie.

Automobile dealer, later President of Hub Oil – Beard Oil Company, Leo Beard and his wife Glenna, bought the home in 1951. Beard was in the Lincoln Mercury automobile business at 227 South Main, currently Listening Ear, and later at 509 North Mission, now Mt. Pleasant Floor Covering, and in the oil marketing business first at 515 North Mission and later at 5644 East Pickard. Here the Beards raised sons Mark and Leonard as well as daughter Kathy,

When the Leo Beards moved to Clare in the 1980s, the house was sold to their son Mark and his wife Linda.

221 North Kinney was built in 1884 by William and Mary Cutler, who sold to Stratton Brooks in 1893, who sold the following year to Daniel and Emma McLachlan, who lived there until 1926, when the house was sold to Morrison and Dain's Builder's Supplies, 221 West Michigan, co-owner Fred S. Dains. The Dains sold in 1935 to contractor Chester A. Welsh and his wife Winifred.

Oilfield lease operator and amateur photographer Walter J. Deibel and his wife Florence Muth bought the home in the late 1930s and here they raised sons Walter John and Charles A. were raised. Walter Deibel died in 1946 and his wife in 1953, when son Charles A. and his wife Marge moved into the house. A few months later, the address would become famous when Marge appeared on the Gary Moore television show and Moore said "You seem like a nice lady. Why don't we all get together and send Mrs. Charles Deibel a nickel." In the ensuing weeks, nearly $8,000 in nickels arrived in town for the Deibels.

Subsequent owners of the address were Broadway Theater Manager Kent Ward; CMU professor Leland Chambers and his wife Marlene; and Ward Theater projectionist Jess Davis and his wife Ivah, secretary bookkeeper for Dr. L. L. Davis.

In 1983, Richard and Mary Alice Bellinger bought the two-lot property, built on lot 4, immediately to the south of this address, *left in photo above*, at **217 North Kinney** and later sold 221 to Allan Kilar and Jo Willson, who in turn sold in 2006 to Gregory P. Smith.

Renters of **221 ½ North Kinney**, an upstairs apartment, have through the years included; Rush Funeral Home mortician John Morin; J. C. Penney employee Thomas Claerr and his wife Christine of Isabella Bank & Trust; and Michigan Oil & Gas News magazine editor Scott Bellinger and his wife Lori Rogers, an English instructor at CMU.

321 North Kinney was built in 1889 by Isabella County Savings Bank's Elton J. VanLeuven and his wife Elizabeth. Elton J. died in September of 1930, but VanLeuven family would retain ownership of the property until 1942, when it was sold to retiring Massachusetts Institute of Technology professor Dr. Floyd Armstrong, who retired here with his wife Olive. Dr. Armstrong, a world-noted economist, was raised in Gladwin, Michigan, and was a graduate of Central Michigan Normal (forerunner of CMU)) and University of Michigan, where he was a professor of economics until his 1916 appointment as Assistant Professor of Political Economics at MIT. He advanced to full professor at MIT before his retirement. He later received an Honorary Doctor of Laws degree from Central Michigan University. Olive Armstrong died in 1962, followed by Dr. Floyd in 1966.

In 1967, the house became home to Gerald R. "Jerry" Sheahan and his wife Dorothy. Jerry owned the bar at 615 North Mission, the longtime Rainbow Bar, then worked for Chippewa Beverage Company before becoming owner of the Green Spot tavern at 808 North Mission. In this house they would raise sons Michael, Timothy, Patrick and Jerry as well as daughters Kathleen and Maureen.

In 1970, Jerry put a Santa Claus on the roof, along with a small stable in the yard and some lights on a few bushes. He won third prize in the city's Christmas decorating contest. Thus a legend was born. The Dorothy and Jerry Sheahan's, *right in candy cane distributing gar*b, annual ever growing Christmas decoration extravaganza became a Mt. Pleasant 42 year tradition and tourist attraction. In 2012, the Sheahans retired the display.

601 North Kinney above in 1906 Built in 1880s, on a lot deeded to Kinney's daughter Bertha Lewis, *see 326 North Fancher page25,* at the time of construction. William West and his wife Mary A. bought the home early in the 20th Century and, after his 1922 death, she lived there until 1940 when she sold to independent oilman George Scheid, manager of Columbia Oil Company and his wife Marie, who raised daughters Catherine, *deceased in 1997*, Barbara and Virginia there, *left in 1988*. George Scheid died in 1990 and Marie, a founding member and enthusiastic supporter to the Mt. Pleasant Area Historical Society, died in 2000.

In 2007, owners Michael and Marcia Brockman received the City of Mt. Pleasant Community Improvement Award for their extensive remodeling of the stately home, *right in 2012.*

604 North Kinney above in 1989 Built in 1885 by Mt. Pleasant pioneer merchant and civic leader John A. Kinney. Kinney was born in Clyde Township, St. Clair County, Michigan, in 1837.

In 1854, his father, Arnold Kinney, one of Michigan's early pioneers employed at various times by the government to build roads through the state, bought 320 acres near what was to become Mt. Pleasant. John worked for his father's lumber interests from age 12, and may have been David Ward's companion who stayed overnight with Mt. Pleasant's first settler John Hursh here in 1855, as they looked over their respective timber properties. Kinney, now a lumberman, returned to the Mt. Pleasant area in 1863 with a crew of ten men to cut practically all the timber and make the Kinney property suitable for cultivation.

Since there was no store in Mt. Pleasant goods had to be bought in from Isabella City, nearly two miles north and across the Chippewa River. In 1863, Kinney bought the log cabin at the corner of Main and Broadway and brought in goods by ox-cart and canoe to open the first mercantile enterprise in town, *see map, right.*

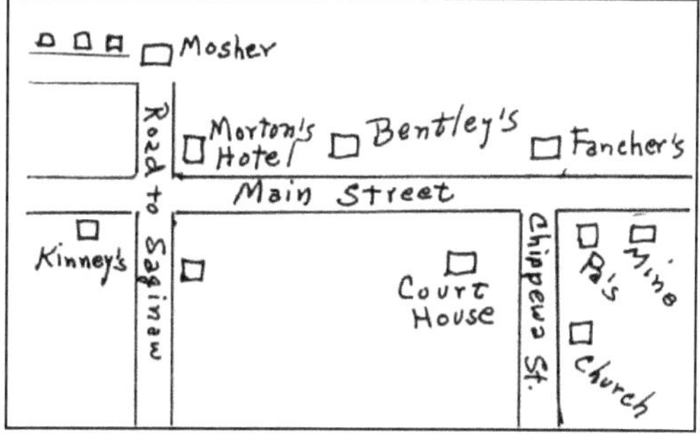

The "Blunt" post office, four miles south, was transferred to Mt. Pleasant and Kinney was the first postmaster, even though the name was not changed to Mt. Pleasant until later. Nelson Mosher was appointed deputy postmaster and Cass Mosher was Kinney's assistant in the store, since Mosher's home was a block away, where the "road to Saginaw", now Broadway, would eventually push through to the Chippewa River and

West Side of town. In 1865, Kinney sold the store and returned to his home in Clyde Township, where he acquired a considerable amount of property and over the years served as Township Treasurer of Clyde and was nominated, but refused, State Congressional offices from that area twice.

In 1877, he returned to Mt. Pleasant and made the Kinney Addition to Mt. Pleasant and the Kinney 2nd Addition in 1884. In 1882, the first Kinney School was built in the 800 block of North Kinney, named in honor of John's civic activities and his addition to the city. The June 19, 1885, *Enterprise* announced Kinney's recent residence plans for Mt. Pleasant with the item: "Mr. John Kinney is building a new dwelling at the corner of Kinney and Andre avenues. It will be 50 x 35 on the ground, two stories high and will contain when finished 18 rooms." In 1914, Kinney subdivided the original Kinney Addition to plat the Kinney and Richmond Addition, see *Appendix 1.*

Kinney and his wife Margaret lived in the house at 604 North Kinney Street until 1918. In 1886, when an "Orphan Train" brought thirty-four orphaned and abandoned children to Mt. Pleasant, the Kinneys were among the local families to adopt one, since four of their five natural children: Arnold, Nettie, Laura, Bertha and Marion had either grown and left home or were deceased. The adopted son, Lester, drowned.

In 1918, failing health apparently forced John and Margaret to sell the house to James and Laura Porterfield and move in with their daughter and son-in-law Bertha and W. E. Lewis, *see 326 North Fancher*. In November, 1919, at age 82, John Kinney died at the Lewis home.

In 1920, the house sold to Hugh A. and Mary McClaren and in 1921 to Edward and Annie Axtell. For a number of years the spacious home was divided into apartments. In 1972, for instance, residents included: Farm Bureau Insurance Agent Thomas D. Carter and his wife Martha, Lease Management clerk Chris L. Henne, CMU secretary Shirley Monton, and, CMU Speech and Drama instructor William E. Valle.

For another period, the house was home to a women's shelter.

The present owners are restoring the home, *right in 2012*, to its original single-home style.

803 North Kinney A pleasant robin's egg blue paint accentuates this house at the northwest corner of Kinney at Palmer streets, built in 1905, according to official records. The home was purchased from the John Kinney estate by Charles and Madge Quinlan in 1925. Over the years the home was occupied by: Ralph H. Dawson, oilfield welder; Archie Boling, oilfield rigger, and his wife May; and, the longest occupant, Benjamin W. Machuta of the oilfield service company Dowell, with his wife Ruth, who raised children Gloria J., Carla, S., Marsha J., William J., Michael P., Mark A. and twins Christopher and Cary. It remains a private residence.

A charming feature of the home is a birdhouse in the tree, left of center above and left here in detail, exactly replicating the main house in both architectural detail and color.

211 North Lansing was built in 1888 by William Taylor, who sold in 1917 to William Cooper, who sold in 1919 to Frederig Baumgart.

The home's quest for a longtime owner ended in 1920, when it was purchased by salesman Charles John Campbell and his wife Rose, who married in 1917. Here they brought daughters Margaret, Marian, Mary C., Charlotte and Dorothy, as well as sons Robert Charles into the world. Charles J. Campbell, an oilfield supply salesman, died in 1938, leaving young Rose with a family of seven.

Rose was born in 1893 to Patrick and Margaret Donovan in Pat's Donovan House hotel at the northwest corner of Broadway and Main Streets, predecessor of the Park Hotel, which would stand until the early 1950s. A lifelong resident of Mt. Pleasant, she graduated Sacred Heart Academy in 1910 and Central State Normal with a teaching certificate in 1912. She had a long career at the Mt. Pleasant State Home and Training School, retiring as a cottage supervisor.

In 1986, she sold the house to son Charles Campbell and his wife Betty, who lived next door at 215 North Lansing until failing health put Rose in the Isabella County Medical Facility, where she succumbed in 1993.

Charles and Betty Campbell now reside here.

304 North Lansing This modified early example of the Colonial Revival style home shows the open-eave influence of the Craftsman era was built in 1885 by Preston S. Fancher and his wife Cora. The house was sold in 1919 to Thomas Battle, who sold in 1926 to Chester Gorham.

From 1946 until 1963 the house was owned by William B. Inglis and his wife Virginia.

The Owens family sold in 1956 to longtime resident Nowland Plumbing and Heating Company owner Richard S. Nowland and his wife Edna. Richard Nowland ran his business on-site and the Nowlands lived here with their children Shirley, Thomas, Pam, Jack and Jon. Edna Nowland died in 1959 and in 1966 Richard Nowland sold to David and Nancy Horrie, who in turn sold in 1969 to Robert and Eileen Strauss, who in turn sold in 1973 to Stanley and Adrienne Walters.

In 1976, the home became the property of Yung and Ok Soon Yung, who sold in 1977 to John w. and Stella Coles, whose improvements on the home earned the 1981 Mt. Pleasant Community Improvement Award Third Place. The Coles sold the house in 1986 to Arthur G. and Nancy A. Behr, who in turn sold in 1993 to Jay and Carol Lancot, who assigned it to Jay Properties.

Jay Properties sold to Elizabeth Domine in 2005.

Over the years, renter occupants of the house have included retired accountant John D. Eckersley, retiree R. C. Balinbaugh, student Jane J. Taylor and student Cheryl DeKaw.

504 North Lansing was built by Samuel Gruett, a lifelong Isabella County resident who, after graduation from Carlyle University at Carlyle Pennsylvania, became supervisor of boys at the Mt. Pleasant Industrial School. After five years he was named manager of the farm, a position he held for 28 years, He continued with the Mt. Pleasant Home and Training School when the facility changed from federal to State of Michigan hands in 1934 and retired in 1945.

Gruett sold this house in 1906 to Wilber Preston, who in turn sold the following year to Lizzie and William Diehl. The Diehls sold in 1908 to Burkley Bump, who in turn sold to Royal and Nancy Peak in 1910, who sold to Garrett and Ellen Vanwie in 1911. In 1917, Glen Riley bought the home and sold it in 1920 to James and Emma Manley.

The Manleys sold to oilfield casing contractor Elmer T. "Tiny" James and his wife Mary Louise, who became the home's longest owners. In the early 1940s, "Tiny" James (a sardonic nickname because of his large size) became a taxi cab owner in Mt. Pleasant and still later an auctioneer. In the 1950s and 1960s, his used merchandise barn at the south end of Washington Street at Broomfield Road south of Central's campus enabled many an arriving college student to outfit their new apartment or dorm room with all manner of living accouterments, probably bought by Tiny from students departing at the end of the previous school year. Elmer T. "Tiny" James died in 1990 and Mary Louise followed in 1994.

In 1994, Richard M. Stanton Jr. and his wife Kathryn bought the house and sold it in 2001 to Jonathon and Amanda Jakubowski.

304 North Main – The oldest surviving home in Mt. Pleasant, at the time of the 1963 celebration of the town's 1863 platting, *above,* was the house at the northeast corner of Chippewa and North Main,.Built by Dr. E. Burt, the house was sold to William W. Preston and his wife Mary when they arrived here in 1863 from upstate

In anticipation of the Homestead Act of 1862, William Preston's son Albert Preston, and son-in-law Samuel Woodworth had come to Isabella County in search of bargain land. Samuel Woodworth's wife Ellen was Isabella County's first schoolteacher.

At the urging of Albert and the Woodworth's when they heard of a town being platted called Mt. Pleasant, Willam and Mary Preston, with son Wallace and daughters Celia and Emma, moved to the fledgling settlement in this house just north of the new wooden county building. Celia marrid E. H. Bradley on October 10, 1865 in the first wedding ceremony performed in Mt. Pleasant.

Shortly thereafter, another Preston daughter, Althea, Mrs. Isaac A. Fancher, and her lawyer/surveyor husbancd moved to Mt. Pleasant from a law practice in Wisconsin . The Fanchers bought three lots directly across Main Street to the west of this house, *see map on page 43.*

This house was demolished to allow northern expansion of the Isabella County Courts House and office complex in the 1980s.

309 North Main might well be called the "home of longevity for its occupant/owners" The house was built on land that was part of property purchased by Isaac A. Fancher, *right,* from Morton brothers in 1865. Fancher lived until the age of 101.

From 1904, it was the home of Dr. Sheridan Ellsworth Gardiner, who graduated from the Medical College of Philadelphia in 1893 and practiced medicine in his native New York state before coming to Mt. Pleasant and establishing offices above Dittman's Shoe Store, *133 East Broadway,* in 1898. In 1944, the office was moved to his home. A 1956 newspaper article announced he was determined by the American Medical Association to be the oldest active medical practitioner in the United States. He made house calls throughout the county until he was 70 and house calls in the city until he was 80. After that he focused on the work of an oculist.

Gardiner's wife, *left in the photo to the left*, the former Blanche Irish, died in 1954 and her niece, Dorothy Irish, *center,* who had come to live with them in 1927 and remained as Gardiner's assistant. Blanche died in 1954. In 1956, S. E. Gardiner married Dorothy. He died at home, at 94 years of age, November 23, 1959, having actively practiced medicine until just a few weeks before his death. Dorothy Irish-Gardiner died in 1961.

In 1962, the house became the property of Margaret Brail and Mary Florence Fox, who sold in 1963 to Verda Marie Davis, a single working mother of four and sister to Mt. Pleasant's first Chief of Police Vernell E. Davis, who served in that position from 1945 to 1959. Verna Marie Davis lived here with her mother Magdalena, widow of Homer Davis, and Magdalena's sister Edith. After the 1963 death of Verda's aunt Edith Hodges, Verda's uncle Leon L. "Jim" Hodges, *below,* also came to live here.

This is where the third long-lived resident of the house comes on the scene.

Leon Hodges was born near Cleveland, Ohio, in December, 1865, and came to Mt. Pleasant in 1888, where he was an engineer for the Gorham Brothers Company, maker of veneers and baskets, where he worked for 30 years. In his later years, he was manager of the Commercial Building, *126-128 East Broadway*. He died in 1966, shortly after his 101st birthday.

Magdalena E. Davis died at 85 years old The house remained under the ownership of Verda Marie Davis *(later Gwaltney)* until her 2007 death. Verda Marie married widowed contractor Charles Oakley Gwaltney in 1978, formerly of Indiana, and they lived in this house until his 1999 death.The property remained in the Charles and Verda Marie Gwaltney Trust until 2009. In 2010, the house was sold to the City of Mt. Pleasant Economic Development Department.

In 2011, the home has been completely transformed into the Jean Prout Trust's Ginkgo Tree Inn Bed and Breakfast and River Bluff Bistro, an establishment lending grace to the old neighborhood and hoping for the same longevity as the previous occupants of the house.

306-328 North Main The three apartment houses, two wood frame and one brick, were built to meet the 1930s Mt. Pleasant housing crunch prompted by the oil "boom" following the 1928 discovery of the Mt. Pleasant Field. All three structures were demolished to make room for the expansion of the Isabella County Building complex.

In 1947, renters of the apartments included: **306 -** oilfield worker Clarence E. Glass, his wife Edna F. and Monte L., a radio technician; **308** – vacant; **310** – Mrs. Anna Estabrook; **312** – Isabella County Deputy Sheriff Ralph Langworthy and his wife Grace; **314 -** William J. Coughlin; **316** – Mrs. Edna B. Maxwell; **318** – oil well driller Albert C. Hawkins and his wife Emma R.; **320** – Harold Woodin, his wife Blanche and daughter Norma Jean; **322** – Harold Chamblin; **324** – trucker Carey Robinson, his wife Lucille, daughter Colleen and son Carey; **326** – toolmaker Walter Scott Westbrook and his wife Vada *(the author's grandparents)*; and **328** – mechanic Carl G. Merrifield, his wife Clara and daughter Bonnie L.

330 North Main – In 1953, Carey and Lucille Robinson pose in front of their apartment house with infant granddaughter Valerie, daughter of Robert and Colleen Robinson-Campbell.

The important part of this photo for this book, however is the house in the background, which was occupied at the time by traffic manager Porter H. Pitts and his wife Helen. The house was razed in the late 1970s to make room for an overflow parking lot for Island Park.

404 North Main This address was originally the 1880s site of a hotel/rooming house named the Peninsular House, operated by J. N. Vancise. In 1898, the Peninsular House was razed and on the spot George H. and Harriet Day built the sprawling house, *above shortly after*. The Days, *below*, owned the Hotel Bennett, having begun their experience in hotel management in 1888 at the Coddington House on Normal Street. They purchased the Hotel Bennett in 1892 and, according to the 1906 booklet *Faces and Places Familiar, Mt. Pleasant Michigan,* "soon made it one of the most popular hotels in Michigan."

George H. Day died in 1922 and Henrietta in 1931.

The Henrietta Day Estate sold the home to Robert and Elizabeth Aylswort in 1934, who sold it to Leo and Ruth Brandell in 1946. Through a succession of eight owners since 1947, the structure has been primarily used as an apartment house, returning to the location's root utility.

418 and 420 North Main are what the author likes to call "architectural cousins" to describe two or more house built with the same design that may or may not have been altered in the aftermath. Some of these architectural cousins are built side by side as mirror images of each other while others, like these, are identical, with the exception of slight differences in the front porches. Both 418 and 420 were built about the same time, during the spurt of home building in the north end of Mt. Pleasant that accompanied the industrial growth there because of the 1879 arrival of the Pere Marquette Railroad depot on North Main Street.

420 North Main, left, was built first, in 1885, by Michael M. Farrell. In the 1920s, the house was owned by shoe cobbler Louis Shauger and his wife Gladys. From the mid-1930s until 1994 the house was owned by carpenter Clarence R. Wince and his wife Josephine R. Clarence Wince died in 1992 and Josephine followed in 1994. The couple was childless.

Since 1994 the house has been a rental, first under the ownership of off-premise owners Thomas Gross and, since 2005, Theodore and Sarah Carson

418 North Main, right Apparently Denis Ryan liked the looks of the house built in 1885 next door at 420, so he built one just like it in 1899. The house was owned in the 1920s to the 1940s by Theodore and Katherine Stockman. From the late 1930s until the late 1950s, the home was owned by restaurant owner Glenn Hammond and his wife Ina. Subsequent owners were Gould Drug Store pharmacist Edwin A. Gillhooley and his wife Sylvia, followed by CMU graduate student John Douglas Mack, then Mt. Pleasant Center for Human Development's Bruce Homblade and his wife Glorian.

Later the house became property of the City of Mt. Pleasant and since 1997 has been in private absentee ownership and used as a rental property first by Ross and Rennae Nugent and, since 2000, by Kelly Miller of Harbor Springs, Michigan.

608-612 North Mission Street was part of Claude and LuLu Day's tract before being added to the City of Mt. Pleasant and the farmhouse survived the transition of dirt Mission Road to United States Highway 27 and, after the highway moved east to become a freeway, returned to Mission Street as Business U.S. 127.

In that distant past when U. S. 27 was two lanes, the area now occupied by Central Plumbing Center, *right above*, saw tourist cabins dotting the east side of Mission, *right*, while the house at **610,** *below,* looked pretty much as it does now.

In 1945, Claude and LuLu Day's son George Day, who grew up in Mt. Pleasant and left to establish a machine shop in Bermuda during World War II, returned to Mt. Pleasant after the war to establish this electrical repair business. Day died in 1989 but the business still operates under the same name, though word "Day", which used to sit atop "Electric", has been removed from the sign. At 616, Dick Switzer operated a barber shop for 42 years. The shop is called Woody's in 2012.

In 1982, the Days sold to William Batchelder and Clair Lapham, who sold it the same year to Fred Motz.

410 North University, right, is a nearly identical twin to a Mt. Pleasant "brick" home nine blocks away at 510 South University. This one was probably built by William and Jane Chatfield in 1884. From 1920 to 1954, it was owned by insurance man M. D. Rand and his wife Kathryn. M. D. Rand died in 1922, leaving Katharyn to live here until her 1952 death. In 1953, the house was sold to carpenter Charles G. Yost and in 1963 to Central Accounting and Tax Service secretary Ruby Lentz. In 1972, Kirkey Electric employee Geraldine Bird moved in, taking ownership in 1994 and transferring it in 1996 to the Geraldine Bird Trust. Matthew S. Chase bought it in 2005.

414 North University, left, was the property of the Salinda D. Whitney family from 1884 until 1908, when this building was built as a daughter church of the Baseline Road Zion Luthern Church congregation, known as the Trinity Lutheran Church. In 1938, the congregation was folded into Zion when the Baseline building was moved to 708 East Maple. The building was then sold to the Owen American Legion Auxiliary, who operated there until 1946. It was then converted to apartments by oil man Frank J, Quinlan who sold in 1975 to Ida Holp. The property went to Hildegard Machuta in 1991, who assigned it to the Hildegard Machuta Trust in 2000. Renter occupants through the years included student Richard L. Amble and his Giant Super Market clerk wife Beverly as well as 10 years later, carpenter Raymond Block; student Diane Welby; and Wentworth & Hovey concrete finisher Jim Wentworth and his wife Sandy.

421 North University was built in 1919 by Ervin D. Morrison and his wife Ella. Ervin, *left*, was prominent in Mt. Pleasant civic life and served as Grand Marshall of the Mt. Pleasant-based Gold Reserve Life Association, a fraternal insurance organization formed in 1901. E.D. Morrison died in 1940. Ella Morrison was known throughout the state for her work with the Christian Science church for 32 years. Though she never had a formal art course, she made a number of fine paintings that brought critical praise. She was a private art instructor to many college students. Ella Morrison died in 1948.

That same year, the house became home to the Morrison's daughter, Phyllis and her husband Norman X. Lyon, *right*, Lyon had come to Mt. Pleasant in 1929 to "help out a couple months at the newspaper" and never left. For the next five decades, Lyon would alternately work for the *Mt. Pleasant Daily Times-News* and forerunners as well as the *Michigan Oil & Gas News* magazine. Phyllis Lyon, an elementary school teacher, died in 1989, followed by Norman X in 1991. Ownership stayed with the estate until 1995, when the house was sold to Mark and Elizabeth Kowalczyk.

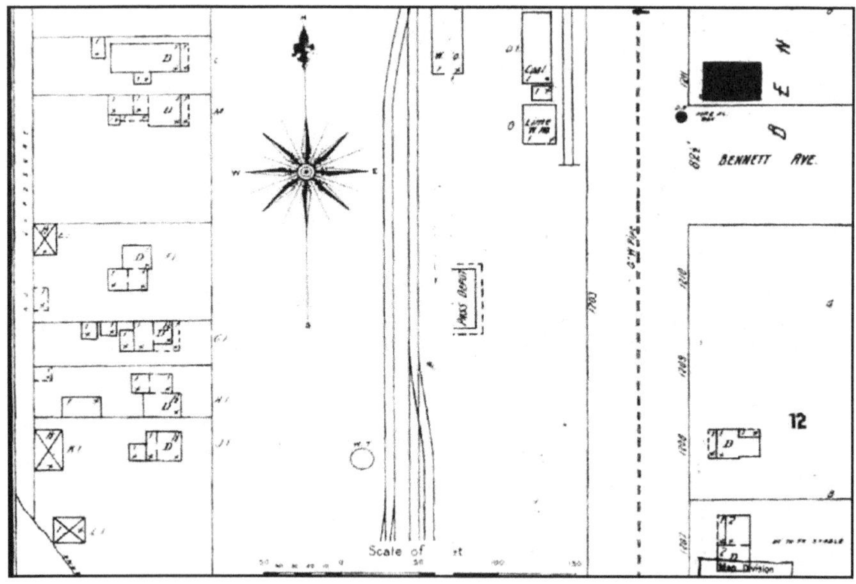

600 – 700 blocks of North Washington, left above, in an excerpt from a 1900 "fire map" of Mt. Pleasant by the Sanborn-Perris Map Company of New York, the row of houses built west of the Pere Marquette Railroad passenger depot was built post-1879, after arrival of the railroad. They likely housed employees of the railroad and other nearby manufacturing venues. Many of these houses, such as the three below, have the Folk National Pyramidal Family design, and probably were erected at the same time as company housing.

603 North Washington, right, has been occupied variously by: Isabella County employee R. A. Rootier, his wife Mildred, along with children Violet, Louise and Lawrence. Latest owner is May 6th Investments.

701 North Washington, left Occupants have included Pullen School janitor Henry Taylor and his wife Ethel. Latest owner is Steve Cotton, who purchased the house in 2002.

703 North Washington, right Occupants have included trucker Earl Hart and his wife Katherine, then later, retiree William F. Green and his wife Adelia. Latest owner is the Richard Tilmann Trust.

East Side
(East of Main Street to Mission)

East:
Andre,
Bennett, Broadway,
Cherry, Chippewa,
Gaylord,
High, Illinois,
Lincoln, Maple,
Michigan,
Palmer,
Pickard, and
Wisconsin Streets

104 East Andre, now 512 North Main, was built in 1879 by H. Edward Deuel, *right below*. While the name will mean little to modern day Mt. Pleasant residents, since there are no streets or buildings named for him save for the bridge to Island Park, nor descendants obvious in local directories, Major Deuel's imprint on the city remains indelible.

Like many who would settle in Michigan after completion of the Erie Canal, Deuel was born in upstate New York, Genesee County, in the mid-1840s. He enlisted in the Union Army at age 18 and went off to battle in the Civil War, returning in August 1865 to marry Celia C. Benedict in New York.

In 1871, he moved to Saginaw, Michigan, where he entered the contracting business for the Pere Marquette Railroad. Eight years later, the Pere Marquette built a spur line to Mt. Pleasant from Coleman, bringing Mt. Pleasant "out of the woods" as noted area historian the late John Cumming was wont to say. Deuel built his home across Main Street just east of the original Pere Marquette depot. It was alongside the supply road that would become the widest street in town, to accommodate freight wagons approaching and leaving the depot, when Cornelius Bennett made his addition to the village in 1882 and named the thoroughfare Andre Street.

H. Edward Deuel was the 11th – 1903-05, 15th – 1909-10, 17th – 1912, and 19th – 1914-1915 Mayor of the City of Mt. Pleasant. The flatland known alternately as Fancher's Meadows, Fancher's Flats and Fancher's Grove, served by a wooden bridge, was purchased by the City in 1909. A canal was dug at the west side of the newly acquired lands and Island Park was born. The wooden bridge was replaced by a cement span bridge and was moved to the southwest boundary of the park, to become known as the Oak Street Bridge. Deuel pushed for a grandstand and racetrack for the new park and persuaded the Isabella County Fair to move there, where the annual Fair took place for decades. He is also credited as one of the prime movers in getting Nelson Park, Mt. Pleasants oldest, added to the town.

He was elected commander of the Northern Michigan Soldiers and Sailors Association, the Grand Army of the Republic, and as such hosted the Fort Sheridan Civil War veterans' weeklong reunion at the new Island Park in 1909, a tradition continuing until the outbreak of World War I. Deuel served in that war as the local Deputy Marshall in charge of Food Distribution.

At his death at 92 years of age in 1937, having been preceded in death by his wife in 1923 and a daughter Clara in 1907, Major Deuel was survived by his remaining daughter Kitty Granville of Saginaw, seven grandchildren nine great-grand children and one great-great-grandchild.

He was a Mason for 65 years and helped organize the Mt. Pleasant Masonic Lodge.

He was also one of the oldest Mt. Pleasant residents, the last Grand Army of the Republic veteran in Isabella County, and for many years was asked to recite Abraham Lincoln's Gettysburg Address at Memorial Day events. Later owner occupants were George Byers and his wife Kittebelle and daughters Jeanne B. and Marilyn B. The Byers family were followed by truck driver Bruce Armstrong and, his wife. The house was split into apartments, remaining a rental property since the 1960s.

H. Edward Deuel's grave Marker at Mt. Pleasant's Riverside Cemetery with the Grand Army of the Republic Civil War Monument in the background. Phoito courtesy Hudson Keenan.

301 East Andre was built in 1879 when the Pere Marquette Railroad came to town. In 1919, the house was owned by William Matier and in 1926 the widowed Flora Bradley lived there, then decorator Harold Beckley and his wife Clara, then truck driver Orville Long and wife Iva. In the mid-1930s oilfield driller Merl Myers and his wife Jessie bought the house and following Jessie's 1971 death son Paul J. "Jake" Myers, an oilfield equipment salesman, lived there until his 1995 death. The house was sold in 1996 to Michael Hutchinson who in turn sold it in 1997 to Robert Paul.

306 East Andre Built in 1914 by Timothy Sullivan the house was the home of A & P Manager Mark A. Dolbur and his wife Emma in the late 1920s, then Exchange Bank cashier Morris Clark and wife Daisy in the 1930s until restauranteur James Moutsatson and his wife Evelyn bought it in 1947 and raised sons Peter and Eugene, as well as daughter Phyllis there. The house belonged to Dow Chemical's Frank J. McGuire in 1972 and Mary B. Myler in 1978. In the 1980s, it became the home of CMU's Sharon Tilman, a longtime Mt. Pleasant City Commissioner.

309 East Andre, above in 1983, was built in the 1920s. Home of Estella Yeager, it sold to William F. Lowther, an oilfield pumper. After Lowther's 1956 death, the house was bought by Mt. Pleasant State Home and Training School groundskeeper Howard Jones and his wife Mary Lou, employed at the same place. In the 1970s, Stanley and Joyce Pridgeon purchased the home, where they raised their children. Stan was also an employee of the Mt. Pleasant State Home and Training School, later with various name changes including the Mt. Pleasant Center, while Joyce worked in the Mt. Pleasant High School cafeteria.

The photo above came from the Pridgeons to show the house before remodeling The left photo shows the house in 2012.

311 East Andre Built by millwright F. James Render and his wife Grace in 1919, the home was a boarding house in the mid 1930s, later owners included: Arthur S. Brown; Roy's Magento's Milo Elliott and his wife Kay; Mary Billington; Richard and Barbara Grace in the late 1960s to late 1970s and more recently David and Debora Andrews.

313 East Andre The house was built around 1889 and was the longtime home of Pere Marquette Railroad Freight Agent Clifford S. Clark and his wife Bertha. Clifford died in 1957 at age 77 and his wife followed in 1970 at age 91. Since that time the address has been listed variously as "student housing" amd "rental property" in city directories.

308 East Andre The house was built in 1903 by Timothy Sullivan, later owned by George W. Schooley and in 1926 was owned by Estella Yeager and rented by truck driver John W. Showalter and his wife Rosetta, then by oilfield rig builder Clarence Ernest and his wife Esta in the late 1930s. Myron "Monk" Huggins, a crude oil purchasing representative for Roosevelt, later Leonard, Refineries and his wife Mary bought the home in the late 1940s. After Myron's 1994 death, Mary lived there three more years before selling to Cathryn Cotter in 1997, who sold to Jonathan D. Kelty in 2005.

314 East Andre Built in 1900 by Thomas J. Fordyce, then owned by janitor Charles Ash and his wife Gladys, the house was bought in the late 1920s by blacksmith James Connor and his wife Ethel. The Connors raised children James D., Frances, Thomas, Lloyd, Leone, Eugene, Mary E., and Dorothy here. The Connor family has owned the home ever since including the adjacent property, *511 North Lansing Street.*

401 East Andre This modified Tudor-style home with cobblestone trimmed first floor, *detailed bel*ow, was built by teacher Asbel "Ash" Upton Ballister and his wife Eleanor in 1904. Ash died in 1921 and his wife followed in 1932, when Bernadette and Angela Mathey acquired the property. In 1966, the house was sold to Robert and Joann Pifer and in 1971 to Thomas and Susan Repp, both Central Michigan University Administrators.

Four owners succeeded the Rapps: Dennis and Karen Kuiper in 1980; Frank and Nancy Ditmars in 1986; Eric and Marie Watson in 1989; and David and Kari Pulver. In 2010, the house was sold to Philippe Giacaloni.

419 East Andre and 601 North Fancher Since Daniel, *right*, and John, *left*, Kane built the residence and store here in 1890, the corner of Fancher and Andre has been the place to live or sell stuff, or both. With the 1879 arrival of the Pere Marquette Railroad and building of a depot at 625 North Main Street, along with the C. Bennett Addition to Mt. Pleasant bordered on the south by Andre, Mt. Pleasant's widest street, the location seemed ideal for a grocery store. The Kane brothers came to the Mt. Pleasant area to settle on a farm in 1882. Tiring of the farm life, Dan and John, with no store experience, decided to try the grocery business here. The business flourished, leading them into expanding into the brick factory business and to build a downtown block.

The Kanes sold to produce dealer William Harrison and his wife La Nora. After Williams death in the late 1920s, La Nora continued to maintain the residence and the grocery store until 1953, when she sold the store to Louis DuHamel, The house has seen a succession of owners and renters since. The store building has variously housed a party store, offices of Bob Acker's Farm Bureau Insurance Agency, the *Michigan Oil & Gas News* magazine, Eight-Cap, the Isabella County Home Builders Association and now Alberta McBride's management offices.

701 East Andre was built in 1905 by Marion E. Kinney-Vanbenschoten, youngest daughter of pioneer Mt. Pleasant merchant John Kinney, *see 604 North Kinney.*

Apparently, Kinney gave each of his offspring property and possibly a home when they got married and stayed in Mt. Pleasant, as with daughter Bertha, see *601 North Kinney.*

In 1919, the house was sold to John S. Caple, who in turn sold it to Orwin and Minnie Raymond in 1921.

The Raymond estate sold in 1937 to Dr. Phillip R. Johnson and his wife Dorothy, who sold in 1940 to Fred Axtell.

In 1947 carpenter Harold W. Hill, his wife Zelpha bought the home and remodeled it in 1950. Here, the Hills raised Annis, Judy, Bill and Kathryn. Harold W. Hill died in 1978 and his wife Zelpha followed in 1991.

In 1995, Kathryn Hill-DeLorenzon-Leiter, with husband Timpthy J. bought the house, her childhood home, and continue to live there.rilyn.

113 East Bennett was built in 1906 by Ward and Maude Kennedy who sold to carpenter John Scharer and his wife Mae in 1913, whose daughter Mary Ellen sold in the 1940s to Dow Chemical retiree Leo Searles and his wife Ethel Mae. The Searles family sold to James S. Lombard, Jr. and his wife Mary Lea S. in 1983, who in turn sold to Walter J. Auger, Junior in 1987. Auger sold in 1996 to Herbert and Janis Voege.

219 East Bennett This gambrel-roofed house was built in 1889 by Charles and Frances M. Forbes and was sold to Floyd Struble in 1908, who in turn sold in 1912 to Jacob and Sarah Martin. Dennis and Caroline Shanahan bought the home in 1916 and sold in 1919 to David and Anna Fisher. The Fishers sold the house in 1926 to Harris Milling Company's William O. Cotter, whose widow teacher Mabel O. Cotter owned the home until her 1972 death, when it was sold to Tom and Donna Ervin.

In 1991 Donna Ervin sold to Richard Childs, who sold to Curtis Buhl, who in turn sold in 2005 to Eric and Carey Pauquette Schalm.

408-412 East Broadway has an indeterminate building date but from 1904 until 1929 was occupied by druggist *(read phamacist)* Albert Gray and his wife Mable. In 1929, Mable sold this house and the one next door at 412 East Broadway, which had been the first library in Mt. Pleasant not in someones home, *shown below in 1920*. The house at 408 and the one next door at 412 East Broadway belonged to Doctor William L. Harrigan, who lived here and used the structure to the east as offices. For a time Dr. Harrigan was the director of the Mt. Pleasant Home and Training School. In 1962, both properties were sold to A & J Laundromat partner Andrew Cascarelli and his wife Eleanor.

411 East Broadway was built in 1889 by Fred and Louise Goldsborough, who sold in 1899 to Amelia Barber.

Veterinarian Doctor Fred F. Cosaul and his wife Stella bought the house and barn in 1904, when Fred joined his fellow Toronto, Ontario, Canada, Veterinarian School graduate, Mt. Pleasant veterinarian John W. Walkington, *with wife Alice below in front of their home at 316 East Broadway in 1923,* in a veterinary practice on his home property. Following Walkington's death 1932, the veterinarian practice came to this address. 316 East Broadway is now a parking lot.

Fred practiced at 411 until the late 1940s and here he and Stella raised daughter Sarah Mae. Stella died in the early 1950s and Fred followed in, 1964, while still living in this house. The house was assigned to Sarah Mae, now Bruder, and her husband John in 1965.

The house then became both the agency and residence to Robert P. Reynolds and his teacher wife Jean M., parents of Yvonne, Judy and Debby, who completed purchase in 1977. In 1988, Reynolds sold house and agency to William Gene Hendrich of Mecosta, who maintained offices here until the early 2000s. The house was vacant for a number of years before a mid-2012 fire caused its demolition.

Alice and John Walkington photo, left, courtesy of Hudson Keenan

502 East Broadway looking south on Fancher is shown above with dirt streets as Dan Johnson, left, and helpers drive cattle to the slaughterhouse. Dan Johnson, the cattle driver, had a son Emory, who with partners, opened an IGA store on East Broadway in the 1950s.

The house on the left was known as the old "Dusenbury place" and was built in 1891 by Cyrus H. Thompson and occupied by George A. Dusenbury and family until 1895 when it was sold to Otis E. Luce, a fireman, and his wife Opal, who furnished the above photo to the Mt. Pleasant *Daily Times-News* newspaper.

In 1946, Otis family sold the house to Joseph and Mary DuHamel, *see 512 East Broadway*, who converted it to an apartments house, which it remains to modern times. Tenants over the years have included Central Students, a re-capper for Mt. Pleasant Tire across the street, a dental assistant to Dr. Norman Eifler, a nurses' aide at the Isabella County Medical Care Facility and a nurses' aide at Central Michigan Community Hospital, among others.

503 East Broadway The date of construction of this structure, *below in the early 1900s*, is unknown but it qualified as a Mt. Pleasant Centennial home when the city celebrated the 100th anniversary of its incorporation as a city in 1989. Property ownership records show George Hicks had the place in 1884, followed by Mary J. Curtis in 1890, Martha Taylor in 1904, Katherine Grinnell in 1918 and Timothy Fitzgerald in 1920.

For a time in the late 1920s the house was the home of surgeon Dr. Stewart McArthur of the McArthur-Strange Clinic at 202 Court Street. In 1936, the home was purchased by funeral director Joseph J. Rush and his wife Marie. Joe Rush was a graduate of Cincinnati School of Embalming in 1927 and had worked for eight years in Detroit before coming to Mt. Pleasant. In his 42 years in business in this building, he would make a dramatic expansion in 1949 with the most up-to-date funeral home in town. Here he and Marie would raise sons James, Thomas, and William. Following Joe's 1978 death, the home was sold to Charles and Nancy Lux in 1980 and passed on to their son Charles Jr. and wife Minde, who sold to Baker Bessheen in 2008. The building is now an aromatherapy and massage institute.

516 East Broadway Female boarders pose in front of the DuHamel Boarding House in the late 1930s, *above*, a popular spot for downtown workers and students to call home. Assessment records indicate the house was built in 1874 but the first deed transaction was in 1888 to May Dusenbury-Humphrey. Later the property belonged to David Davidson in 1890; Charles Rush in 1894 until 1920; George and Edith Kniffen in 1920; Clarence Hulse in 1927 and Erma Hammond in 1934.

In 1937, the house was sold to Joseph, Sr. and Grace DuHamel. Grace was owner of DuHamel's Style Shop at 122 East Broadway. Grace DuHamel died in 1995 and ownership of the house, *below*, which continues as a place of apartment rentals, went to David and Bruce DuHamel.

522 East Broadway This property and its neighbor to the east, 524 East Broadway, shared common ownership from the 1800s when the Chattertons owned them until 1938. In 1915, Amorette E. Chatterton sold the lots to Thomas Sampson along with Howard and Harry Chatterton. The Chattertons sold to oil and gas contractor William Gill and his wife May in 1928, whose estate sold 522 to insurance man Floyd A. Seeley, who had both office and residence here,while raising daughter Donna M.

In 1955, the Seeleys sold this house to attorney Ray Markel, who in turn sold to Coleman and Katherine Peters, former business and residence owners of the Campbell Building at 107 North Main. The Campbell Building was where Coleman Peters opened Mt. Pleasants first television sales and service establishment. The building was home to the original Giant Super Market.

Coleman C. Peters, *below in 1943*, was raised in Cheboygan, Michigan, and was the first special representative of HCJB radio station in Quito, Eucador as well as a member of the board of Directors for MarAnatha Bible Conference at Muskegon, promoting Youth for Christ. He was an active member of the First Baptist Church at Broadway and Fancher, then the Strckland Baptist Church. He was also active in the Gideon Society, where he served as Past President from 1947 to 1950.

From 1937 until 1961, he was involved in radio and television in Central Michigan including having a family radio show in the fledgling days of WCEN radio at 112 ½ East Broadway. In 1961, he became a realtor, as did his wife, and after selling the Campbell Building, they moved to this address. Along the way, they raised four sons – Douglas, John, David and Stephen, as well as two daughters, Marilyn and Susan. Coleman died in 1974 and Kathleen followed in 1982.

The house sold in 1983 to J & J Apartments.

524 East Broadway has an indefinite building date but was probably, like it's neighbor to the west, **522 East Broadway**, built under the ownership of Amorette E. Chatterton, who sold to Thomas Sampson along with Howard and Harry Chatterton. The Chattertons sold to oil and gas contractor William Gill and his wife May in 1928, whose estate sold in 1938 to chiropractic physician Dr. George C. Batson and his wife Audrey, who used the building for offices, also for the Batson Apartments. In the Batson years, renters included Flamingo Bar's H. A. Corbin and Dr. Schmidtmitt,

The east side of the building is shown right as backdrop to the November, 1942, dedication of Mt. Pleasants World War II monument on the south side of Broadway at Kinney Boulevard.

Dr. Batson died in 1974.

More recent owners of the building, now home of Answers Counseling Services and apartments, include John F. Neyer, Lynn R. and Virginia Chamberlain, the Virginia Chamberlain Trust and, since 2009, Kim Ellerson.

314 East Cherry In 1884, Scott Partridge sold this and the lot for 305 East High to Bert Parkhill, who in turn sold it to Glen H. and Gladys McGreagor. McGreagor sold it to Joseph P. and Ida M. Carey, who built the house. Carey, *right,* who would head the Central Michigan College Geography Department from 1944-1956, joined the school's faculty in 1925 as an assistant geography professor. He also was president of the Mt. Pleasant School Board, Chair of the City Planning Commission, and served as secretary of the Michigan Oil And Gas Association Oil and Gas Exposition Committee. The exposition drew more than 20,000 people to Mt. Pleasant's Island Park in 1935, hearlding the news that an oil and natural gas exploration and production activity here shielded the town from the financial devastation of the Great Depression. Joseph Carey died in 1968 and Ida followed in 1979, Ida sold the house to Patricia Murphy in 1969, but continued to live there until her death. Murphy sold it in 1981 to Warren Atkins Brindle.

In 1982, the house was sold to Terry S. and Marcia M. Quast.

318 East Cherry has been home to three stars of the Mt. Pleasant educational system and Central Michigan College/University education and related administration scenes since its erection in 1905, according to City of Mt. Pleasant Assessing Service online software. The property was owned by George Loomis at the time, and then sold to Anna Dean in 1912, then to William and Sue May Anderson in 1917.

In 1920, the house was sold to Mt. Pleasant Superintendent of Schools George E. Ganiard, *right,* and his wife Martha. George Ganiard was born in Concord, Michigan, in 1873 and got his Teachers Certificate at Michigan State Teachers College at Ypsilanti in 1897. He taught in rural and grade schools until 1901, when he took the job of Superintendent of North Adams schools 1901. In 1903, he moved to Milan, Michigan where he was Superintendent until 1907 until 1910, when he became superintendent of Ithaca schools. From 1910 to 1913, he was a newspaper editor in Reed City, before returning to his true calling, education, by accepting the job of Mt. Pleasant Superintendent of Schools in 1914. Along the way, he earned his Bachelor of Science degree from University of Chicago in 1914 and his Masters Degree from University of Michigan in 1929.

Ganiard served as Mt. Pleasant Superintendent of Schools until his January 1939 death at 65 years old. In his honor, all Mt. Pleasant schools were closed the day of his funeral and the newly–built West Side School at the southeast corner of Broadway and Adams streets was renamed for him. George and Martha, *shown left in her region-renowned flower garden,* raised their only child, Louise Ganiard Johnson, of New York, here.

The George Ganiard and garden pictures herein were furnished to Valerie Wolters, coordinator of the Ganiard History Project (*gandiardhistory08@gmail.com*) and by Janine Johnson Wein of Lyme New Hampshire, granddaughter of George and Martha Ganiard.

Ownership remained with the Ganiard family until 1964 but was rented to a couple who purchased the home in 1964, Bernard N. Meltzer and his wife Ida. Bernard N. Meltzer served 40 years as a Central Michigan College/University faculty member and 30 years as Chair of Central's Department of Sociology, Anthropology, and Social Work. During his tenure, social and criminal justice, as well as anthropology were added to the department. He published over three dozen articles and five books during his career, most dealing with the symbolic interactional perspective. His wife, Ida Meltzer, was equally prominent as a Central instructor in the field of Political Sciences and heralded women's rights in such organizations as the National Organization of Women.

Bernard N. Meltzer retired from Central in 1987 and died at 91 in 2008. He and Ida raised two children: daughter Iris Meltzer, holder of degrees in both psychology and public health; and William J. Meltzer, an anthropologist. Daughter-in-law Cathy Malkin is a psychologist and granddaughter Moira Meltzer-Coen is a curriculum specialist with a background in philosophy.

The home, now property of the Bernard N. Meltzer Trust, is pending sale owners at this writing.

625 East Cherry combines a modified French eclectic dormered two story look with the sprawling ranch style home that originated in California in the mid-1930 and rapidly became popular nationwide. The growing dependence on the automobile was a factor, as well as the presentation of a wider façade when this house was built by Charles Clarence Hood for dentist Dr. Eveleth A. Northway and his wife Grace in 1936.

Dr. Northway maintained his dental practice and offices at 1015 East Wisconsin. Together they raised daughter Jan here. E. A. was a Lt. with the U.S. Naval Dental Corps during World War II. In 1971, after several winters of wintering there, the E. A. Northways moved permanently to Scottsdale, Arizona. He had practiced in Mt. Pleasant for 41 years at retirement. E. A. died in Arizona in 1978.

Grace Northway was a 1926 cum laude graduate of Michigan State University and a member of Kappa Kappa Gamma Sorority. In Mt. Pleasant, she served on the board of the St. John's Episcopal Church and several other civic and social committees. Grace returned to Michigan in 1985 to live in Lansing until her 1988 death.

In 1973, the Northway's sold to Charles J. and Claire Pung, who in turn sold it in 1975 to State Court Administrator Jack Crandall and his wife Virginia, an employee of the Shepherd school system.

In 1989, the house sold to Jeff Jakeway and since then has been a rental property.

203 East Chippewa is shown above in 1931 with Central State Teachers College roommates Bessie and Orpha *(last names not available)* and Hazel Boyer posing in front of the original house at this address, built in 1904. The home was owned by George and Julia McKnight, co-owners of McKnight & DuHamel, ladies-ready-to-wear store, at 120 East Broadway, listed in Mt. Pleasant city directories as early as 1926 *(which said George owned a Studebaker)*.

The front porch was enclosed and the house modernized later to give it the more streamlined look of today. The McKnight home continued to house students in part of the home even after George's 1958 death. As late as 1972, the year of her death, Julia McKnight was renting to Christine Matrauga, a Central Michigan University student and Giantway Department Store clerk. The home remains a private residence.

209 East Chippewa The house was built in 1910 by Bart Greuner, whose widow Hester married one of the McNutt family who was associated with Harris Milling Company. Originally there were servant's quarters in the basement.

After the family no longer occupied the structure, it became offices for doctors Anderson, McGinnis and Carson. Dr. McGinnis sold it to Ken and Ruth Folkert who returned the woodwork to its original finish and restored the marble inlaid bathroom tiles. Chamberlain and Havens Law offices occupied the building in 1992, when the home was included on the Mt. Pleasant Area Historical Society Christmas House Walk, *above.* The structure is now the headquarters of McBride Quality Care.

215 East Chippewa. This gable front double winged "Mt. Pleasant brick" home with gabled porch was built by pharmacist Corey P. Taylor and his wife Nellie sometime during their 1893-1922 ownership of the property. In 1922, the Corey's sold to Ambrose and Alvira Van Horn.

In 1937, the Van Horn's sold the house to insurance and bonds agent Malcomb S. Wardrop and his wife Margaret. Here they raised Malcomb Junior (killed in a plane crash in Kentucky in 1943), Merrie, Robert, William, Daniel and Elvira. Malcomb died in the late 1950s and in 1972, Margaret sold the big house to Central Michigan University Director of Financial Aid John W. Stressman, Junior, and his wife Dorothy. Margaret Wardrop then moved into a small house at the northwest corner of the property, which became ***213 East Chippewa***, *right*, until her 1983 death.

John and Dorothy Stressman raised John W. III, Richard, Steven, Robert, Patricia and Peter at 215. John Stressman died in 1978 and Dorothy followed in 2003, at which time the house was bought by son Steven Stressman and his wife Robin.

301 East Chippewa is the oldest remaining house in Mt. Pleasant. The home was practically new, built about 1865, when the Wilkinson Doughty family gathered on the front porch, *above,* to pose for a photograph with the Doughty Company Wagon out in front. Wilkinson Doughty was a merchant, town trustee, one of the founders of Central Michigan Normal School, now University. Below, the house had five chimneys, wooden sidewalks and a dirt Franklin Street running alongside.

The last Doughty to occupy 301 East Chippewa was Margaret Doughty, *above*, shown on the same front porch about a hundred years after her ancestors bought the house in 1869. Following Margaret Doughty's 1993 death, the house was sold to William Harlow and operated as a bed and breakfast inn for awhile. Later sold to Anne & Colin Alton in 1998, it is now a family residence.

According to Michigan Historical Marker #L223A, placed on the front of the house on the U.S. Bicentennial July 4th weekend in 1976, the house is "a carefully preserved example of balloon frame pioneer architecture" . It was listed as the premier Mt. Pleasant Centennial Home when the city celebrated it's 100 aniversary of incorporation in 1989.

302 East Chippewa was built in 1884 on lot 10 and part of lot 11 of Mt. Pleasant Original Plat by John Hicks and sold in 1903 to Fred and Florence Russell. Fred Russell, *below left*, was born on a farm near Grand Ledge, Michigan, in 1855, where he was raised and taught school in the area while studying law. After admission to the bar, he came to Mt. Pleasant to form a partnership with his brother, Charles T. Russell, in a law firm he served until his 1926 death. He was elected to the Circuit Court Comission and to the office of Justice of the Peace several times. He was also senior partner in the Russell & Foland jewery firm at 125 East Broadway for many years. He married Florence Russell, a former post office employee who came to Mt. Pleasant in 1881 with her parents Tom and Mary Hunt. She was devoted to benevolence work and was president of the Sunshine Society for many years, a member of the Laff-A-Lot Society from its 1940 organization and was a member of the Ladies Supper Club. In 1922, Fred and Florence Russell sold the house to their nephew, insurance and real estate man Walter W. Russell. Walter W. Russell, *right*, was the man who leased the pipeline right of way from Pure Oil's discovery of the Mt. Pleasant oil field in 1928, thirteen miles to the railhead at Mt. Pleasant so that oil from the field could be transported to market. This led to Mt. Pleasant's title "Oil Capital of Michigan". In 1977, the house became Robert and Janet Pulver's Guy's & Doll's Photography

415 East Chippewa This Second Empire Victorian-era home was built in 1874 by John D. Doughty, a printer by trade, who came to Mt. Pleasant in 1872 to take over publication of one of the village's newspapers, *The Enterprise*, which he bought upon the death of its owner, Albert Fox. At the time he was courting Eva Craig Graves, of Warsaw, Kentucky. In 1873, he promised to build Eva "the most beautiful home in town" as an inducement to come to Mt. Pleasant.

In 1875, the printing office and all its fixtures were destroyed by fire. There was no insurance. Doughty ordered a new press from Detroit and set up office in the parlor of his home, issuing the next issue of *The Enterprise* on its regular day the following week. The newspaper was printed from here until new offices were built. The marks on the floor made by the printing press have been preserved by each succeeding owner. John and Eva edited the newspaper together and she, a devout suffrage worker, brought Susan B. Anthony to town and was her host when she came here to lecture on the suffrage cause. The sherrif locked them out of the courthouse and Anthony gave her lecture at Carr & Grangers's Hall downtown on March 17, 1879.

John Doughty owned *The Enterprise* until 1885, when he sold to A. S. Conant to pursue other business interests until his 1907 death.

For more than 40 years, the 1920s to 1960s, the house was owned by the an oilman Charles Wildermuth and family. After Charles death, Ethyl Mae Wildermuth managed to make her money last until her 1989 death, selling the back portion of the property in the 1940s to Union Rotary Drilling Company's Earl Andrews, who built a home at *315 North Fancher. see page 20.*

In 1986 Alan and Diane Shinevar bought the home and painstakingly restored it to it's Victorian era exterior colors and furnished it in 1900-1930 era furniture

Later owners included Jack and Cora Neyer, who bought the house in 1998 and sold it in 2000. The house remains, in 2012, a well maintained and orderly private residence.

503 East Chippewa, above in 1906, was built in 1884 by Ellen Elizabeth Coons and sold in 1902 to Ezra S. Gorham, *right,* Treasurer and co-founder of the Gorham Brothers Company saw mill, lumber, veneer and retail local giant and at the turn of the 20th Century, Mt. Pleasant's largest employer. The house was a duplex and often used by Ezra's brother Chester R. Gorham, *left*, who as president and co-founder of the company, split his time between here and the company's home and headquarters in Cleveland, Ohio, where his family resided, and the Mt. Pleasant operation. Ezra died in 1910 And his wife Mary followed in 1911.

In 1916, ownership of this house then went to Mt. Pleasant trial attorney, former prosecuting attorney and two-term Michigan legislator Frank Dusenbury and his wife Edith E. (Gorham).

Until 1922, ownership of this property and the one next door to the east. *509 East Chippewa*, was common, with the Coons, Gorhams and Dusenburys owning both, *see immediate following pages*.

Here at 503 the Dusenbury's raised son Blair, daughter Marcia and lost infant daughter Anne. Frank R. Dusenbury, *right,* lost his life in a November, 1930, car accident when his car skidded into a tree near St. John's, Michigan. Edith retained ownership of the property until her 1967 death.

Next owners of the property were Everett M. and Marcia (Dusenbury) Rupert, owners of the Sport & Toy store at 115 East Broadway.

The Ruperts sold the house in 1975 to Dorothy Updegraff, who sold in 1989
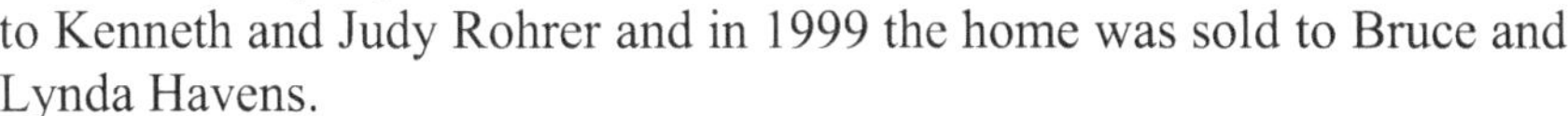
to Kenneth and Judy Rohrer and in 1999 the home was sold to Bruce and Lynda Havens.

Through the years, renter occupants of the home have included Vice President of Roosevelt Oil Company William L. Davis in the late 1930s and early 1940s; Gordon Oil President I. W. "Bucky" Hartman, *see 1002 South Fancher*, and his wife Velma in the mid-1940s; and Bernice Battle, widow of John F. Battle.

The house is shown below in 2012, with a rental property apartment over the garage addressed as *306 South Fancher.*

509 East Chippewa Built in 1884, this house and property shared common ownership with *503 East Chippewa*, pages immediately preceeding, until 1922. Retired farmer Patrick Trainor and his wife Mary bought the home in 1922. Trainors children were daughters Gertrude, Emma, Mrs. Albert Kidd, and Mrs. James Lawler, *no first names given*, along with two sons, Leo and Harry.

Next owners of the home was accountant/oil producer Arthur H. Ledbeter, *right*, who got his start in the oil business as office manager for McClanahan Oil Company in the early 1930s and later was Secretary-Treasurer of Lease Operating Company and his wife Vivian.

Next owners of the house were mail carrier Richard Funnell and his wife Rosemarie, who worked at the Central Michigan University Bookstore.

The story of the Funnell's acquisition of the home, and their longtime envying it from afar,at *801 Mosher Street,* is best told by "Rosie" Funnell's own words in a narrative written especially for this book:

"We bought this house from Mrs. Art Ledbeter in 1970, but really had hoped to buy it about 1952. We would walk by on our way to the

park when my kids were small and always remarked that this house was someday going to be ours.

One day my niece called and said the house was going up for sale since Mrs. Ledbeter was moving in with her daughter Dorothy. We were the third bid on the house. By chance, the first bid found another house and the second couldn't come up with the down payment.

So we bought the house for $3,000 down and $100 a month on land contract. (The Funnells took title in 1988).

Nothing much has changed, (the house is shown right in 1970) except we remodeled the kitchen. All the floors are hardwood and in good shape. Someone before us made the third bedroom into a bathroom upstairs.

We moved in just before Christmas. Mike was in college and came home with a tree ...that was pretty much our Christmas. We had a big bare house for awhile until we hired Aburna "Burnie" Bonnell to come and help us decorate. She helped make it a home. Dick died in 2003.

Our children are Mike, Patrick, Nancy and Gayla."

The Funnell Family in 1999, left to right: Back Row – Dick and Rose Funnell with Joe Vodicka. Second Row – Mike, Jan, Pat, Kim, Marcia, Jason, Patrick, and Amanda Funnell. Beth Funnell, Gina Vodicka, Jill Funnell, Nancy and Bob Vodicka, Gayla Fisher and Paul Funnell.Front Row: - Kevin Fisher with dog, Julayne Vodicka, Matt, Mike and Lee Fisher.

515 East Chippewa Street This side gabled roof, exposed rafter Craftsman-style house with sweeping arched screened windows enclosing the front porch was built in 1920 by Marshall K. Gorham for optometrist Sid G. Thompson and his jeweler wife Gertrude, owners of Thompson Jewelers and Optometrists at 106 East Broadway.

Here they raised son C. E. Thompson. Gertrude Thompson died in 1951 at age 73 and Sid followed two years later in 1953, also at 73 years old.

The house, as well as the business, now Thompson and Son Jewelers and Optometrists, went to son C. Edgar Thompson, also an optometrist, and his wife Bonnie. C. Edgar Thompson died in 1960 at 50 years of age and in the later 1960s, the house sold to Mt. Pleasant Culligan Soft Water Service owner Vernon Lee Kennett and his wife Carole.

In 1978, Alan Weber and his wife Mary owned and were living in the house

Most recently the home belonged to Larry A. and Mary Ann Walsh Miller, who sold to Michael and Elizabeth Hilley early in 2012.

619 East Chippewa This house has been home to two large families since its 1935 construction.

The house was built for Mt. Pleasant merchant Peter F. Breidenstein, partner in Breidenstein and Kane Hardware, 121 East Broadway, and his wife Mary. Here they raised sons John, James and Eugene and daughters Mary and Helen. Mrs. Mary Breidenstein died 1947 at 55 years old, after which Peter continued to live in the house, sometimes with renter/caretakers like Associated Drillers and Producers, Inc. General Manager Robert E. Sole and his wife Helen in the 1950s. Peter Breidenstein died in 1960 at 88 years.

In 1961, another large family, Gould Rexall Drug Mt. Pleasant Store Manager Richard Brandell and his wife Mary Ellen bought the house. Here they would raise daughters Mary, Ann, Kathleen and Carol along with sons Joseph, Richard and James. Later Richard was a pharmacist at Downtown Drugs before overtaken by an extensive illness, fatal in the 1990s.

While raising the Brandell brood, Mary Ellen earned her Doctrate in communications at Central Michigan University, was vice mayor of Mt. Pleasant, had been interim vice provost of international affairs at CMU, assistant to the provost of international affairs and associate dean of the CMU College of Education and Health and Human Services. She also co-chaired the Mt. Pleasant Centennial Committee in 1989 and was Founders Day Chair of the February 11, 2009, Isabella County Sesquicentennial Founders Day celebration. She was 2010 recipient of the John Cumming Isabella County Historical Preservation Award. Mary Ellen Brandell died September 24, 2010. Daughter Kathleen Brandell Mumford now owns the house.

406 East Gaylord Of all the houses in this book, this cement block structure leaves the least doubt as to its dates of construction, since "1908" is inscribed in cement between the upper and lower windows of the main façade. In 1908, Paul Smith and his wife Gillie built the house and in 1912, Isabella County Register of Deeds records show it was assigned to Gillie, Robert R., Leah J., Marshall H., Archie D., Marlet V., and Bennie J. Smith, apparently to keep it "all in the family". This worked for fifty years, until 1962, when Leah J. Smith sold the property to Marshall Bennett, who in turn sold it the following year to Ralph Arthur and Joan Vivian Bock.

Paul Smith died in 1916 and Gillie followed in the late 1940s.

Central Michigan University teachers George A. and Marilyn Zorn bought the house in 1964. In 1996, it was acquired by Rosanne Kappler, who sold in 2001 to Russell T. St. John. In 2005, Ramon R. Beaulien bought the home and sold it to Jackel Properties in 2011.

Through the years, rental occupants of the house have included a number of Central students, besides: ironworker Lawrence E. Keiber and his wife Sarah; Novi Brown; and Mc Farlane Dairy salesman Rudy Bock.

221 East High Street. This Mansard roofed house at the northwest corner of High and Franklin street was built in 1890 by George and Emiline Owen. The Mansard type roof is subtype of the Second Empire style, which closely resembles the Beaux Arts style of eclectic homes, loosely based on 17th and 18th Century French Renaissance models that have distinctive dual-pitched hipped roofs with dormer windows in the steep lower slope. The Second Empire houses are generally smaller, as with this house, and have walls of wood or brick rather than the stone and façade decoration of Beaux Arts homes.

The office building at *500 South Main Street, right,* is a more dramatic Mt. Pleasant example of the Second Empire style. That building was built as a home in 1902 by John Bamborough, who sold to Harper and Zello Blanche Maybee in 1907, who sold to Charles and Amy Hagen in 1921, who sold to John and Amelia Sonneberg in 1927. Attorney Virgil McClintic turned the home into an office building in 1928.

Back now to 221 East High. The Owens sold in 1903 to Mahon and Della Brown. The Browns sold in 1907 to Frank and Jennifer Theirs, who were among the first investors when John Weidman launched the Isabella County State Bank with $30,000 in capitalization.. The Theirs sold to Homer and Elizabeth Derr, who sold to Enos and Mary Crandell, who sold to Mrs. E. L. Stovely and Mrs. Annie Bolton in 1926. Through the 1940s into the 1960s, the home belonged to insurance man Charles F. Dumon and descendants. In 2011, the house was sold to Anthony Smicler.

301 East High, above in 1906, might well be called the home of Central Michigan Normal School/College Presidents. Charles Grawn, right, and his wife Helen built this house at the northeast corner of High and Franklin streets in 1900. He came to Mt. Pleasant from a 15-year position as Superintendent of Schools in Traverse City 1899 when appointed president of Central in 1900. During his 1900-1918 tenure, building of the training school, power plant, gymnasium and science building took place and the campus grew from 11 to 25 acres. Charles Grawn Hall opened in 1915 and remains the oldest building on campus.

Later the address was home to 1918-1939 Central President Dr. Eugene Charles Warriner, left, and his wife Ellen. Warriner's tenure saw two campus fires, an influenza epidemic, the beginning of Bachelor of Arts and Graduate degree offerings at Central, the Great Depression, plus the building of Michigan's first women's dormitory at a normal school and a new athletic field.

Subsequent owners of the home included pharmacist Morris J. and wife Audrey Winslow, as well as Central Teacher Jay H. Shurtliff and his wife Louise.

The house remains a private residence.

305 East High was built in 1884 by Bert H. Parkhill, who came to Mt. Pleasant from Howard, New York, and was connected with the banking business with First National Bank of Mt. Pleasant, then in 1891 he became secretary treasurer of Gorham Brothers Company of Mt. Pleasant. Parkhill brought his new wife, Eleanor, here in 1885 and in this house they raised a son, George, and three daughters; Louise P., Miriam P., and Vera P. Bert Parkhill died in 1928 at 68 years old. Eleanor lived in the house until her 1960 death at 97 years old, when her granddaughter Patricia MacGillivray became owner and lived there until 1977. At the time of her death, Eleanor Parkhill was the oldest member of the First Presbyterian Church of Mt. Pleasant and was an active member of the Women's Christian Temperance Union and the Eastern Star Masonic Lodge, in all of which she participated until illness confined her to her home

Jill Kooiman, assistant Mt. Pleasant City Manager, and her husband bought it and made major renovations, leaving the original woodwork and pocket doors.

Myron and Kristine Georgia lived in and owned the house from 1984 until 2004 when sold to James and Elizabeth Eikren in 2004

The home was included on the Mt. Pleasant Area Historical Society Christmas House Walk. At that time the kitchen featured oak cupboards built from cabinets in the kitchen and dining room. The living room and parlor had original light fixtures and hand painted fireplace pieces. First floor bathroom was added in the 1930s. A back upstairs dormer added post-1977 features two full baths, closets and a laundry.

307 East High was built in 1903 by well known Central Michigan Normal/College/Professor Elizabeth R. Wightman *below*. Her initial teaching took place in the Mount Pleasant public school system before studying at Ypsilanti (Michigan) Normal College, returning to teach art and geography at Central Michigan Normal. Promoted to the rank of professor and head of the Department of Art in 1900, she was faculty advisor to the Art Club. Retiring in 1937, she died in a Detroit hospital in 1940 after a short illness. Elizabeth Wightman Hall, named in her honor, opened in 1948 on the west side of Washington Street at the site of the old athletic field, used until 1930, behind Old Central Hall. Wightman Hall is now home to the Art and Human Environment Studies departments.

The house remained in Wightman family ownership until 1955, when it was sold to popular petroleum landman Alan Gray and his wife Grace. Later owners included: CMU professor Alban W. Coen and his wife Patricia in the 1960s through mid-1980s; Ken W. McCleary and Pamela Weaver in the mid-1980s; and Joseph and Deborah Finck in 1988. For awhile the house ran as a bed and breakfast inn, but it has returned to a private residence. Central Michigan University's Calvin Tormanen and his wife Susan, a Beal City elementary school teacher, bought the house in 1995.

405 East High was built in 1900 by George Loomis and sold in 1905 to Central Michigan Normal School History and Social Studies Department head Claude S. Larzalere, *left*, and his wife Lorena. Larzalere headed the aforementioned departments from 1900 until 1939. He was author of a number of Michigan history and government books both before and after retirement. He died here in 1946.

The house sold to oil and gas leaseman Worth J. Dafoe and his wife Virginia in 1947. Dafoe's sold the home in 1953 to another oilman, Vance W. Orr, Sr. *right*, and wife Emily in 1952.

The Orr's had rented the house across the street at *402 East High* for years before buying the Worth Dafoe home. Here they raised Vance W. Jr., James and Ann. Vance Orr Sr. had come here from Tennessee in 1937 with McClanahan Oil Co. and spent most of his career with McClure Oil and Michigan Oil Company. He was 1985-86 president of the Michigan Oil And Gas Association. He died in 2005 in Crystal, Michigan, which had been his home since selling 405 in the early 1980s. He was preceded in death by his wife and all of their children.

Subsequent owners of the home have included Edward and Marsha Schmidt, as well as Wayne P. Nicholson.

518 East High This Tudor style home with wood cladding and an arcaded wing wall housing with a gable front entrance was built by Charles D. and Emma Brown, who sold in 1934 to Mrs. Etta B. Durfee, Mrs. Durfee died in 1942 and the family retained ownership of the home for a few more years.

In 1950, osteopathic physician Doctor R. A. Northway and his wife Nancy, parents of daughter Jean and sons Robert O., Frank, and Thomas purchased the home. R. A. Northway practiced in Mt. Pleasant for nearly half a century, having come here in 1910 to open a practice in the Dusenbury Building, 113 East Broadway, then the Exchange Bank Building at Broadway and Main, and finally at 233 North Main Street. Two years before his 1956 death, ill health cause him to close the Clinic. Originally from Owosso, Michigan, he was a graduate of Kirksville Osteopathic College in Missouri and had done his post graduate work in ear, nose, and throat in Chicago before coming to Mt. Pleasant. His skill with the treatment of burns and injuries had brought many oilfield workers and accident victims to his care. He also served as Isabella County Coroner for 12 years. Following his 1956 death, his son Mt. Pleasant High School teacher Tom Northway, later with his wife Kathryn, also an MPHS teacher, lived with Nancy until her 1962 death.

In 1963, the house became property of Tom and Kathryn, where they raised Thomas, Patrick and Susan before making their home at a longtime family home in Beulah, Michigan, and selling this home in 1983 to Robert and Carolyn Kennett. The Kennetts sold in 1988 to State Farm Insurance Agent Conrad English and his wife Kimberly A., who sold in 1997 to Roger K. VanHorn and Kay E. Bakker.

Alberta McBride bought the home in 2002 and assigned it in 2006 to the Alberta McBride Trust.

314 East Illinois was built in 1905 by the long-widowed Agnes O'Hara, sister of local hotelier Thomas Bamber, both born in Canada. Pictured at the right are Agnes O'Hara's daughters Celia and Viola shortly after the house construction was completed. Two years after completion of the home, Agnes O'Hara was stricken by rheumatism that left her an invalid. For the next fifteen years, until her 1922 death, surrounded by family in this home, she was attended at all times, in later years living with her now-married daughters Mrs Alex (Viola) Murphy of Milwaukee, Wisconisn and Mrs. Hugh (Celia) Murphy of this address in Mt. Pleasant. In 1923, the property became that of Hugh and Celia Murphy.

Oilfield driller Thurman F. McQuaid and his wife Edwardine, daughter of Hugh and Celia Murphy, bought the house in 1944 and here they raised Thurman F. "Fred" Junior, Mary K., Alice A, Celia *(named for her grandmother)*, and Edward. Thurman McQuaid died in 1973 and his Edwardine followed in 2002.

In 1976, the house was sold to Jess and Gretchen Merrill, who sold in 1989 to Jan and Jill Schray Simons, who have painstakingly returned the home to an almost perfect duplicate of itself as a new house, down to the detail of the decorated verge boards in the front gable, *above*.

320 East Illinois This property was bought in 1901 by Father Thomas J. O'Connor of Sacred Heart Catholic Church, across the street. The home was built in 1903 by Father John A. Crowley of Sacred Heart, probably as a retirement home. It was longtime home of Edward J. Dittmann, *left,* and his wife Bessie. Dittmann was the manager of Dittmann and Son Shoe Company at 133 East Broadway. Born in Reed City in 1873, Edward Dittman lived for a time in Grand Rapids, then attended business colleges in Saginaw and Bay City before moving to Mt. Pleasant in 1895. He became a partner in Dittmann Shoes in 1900 and took over the firm in 1910, Retiring from the firm due to ill health, he died in this home in 1942.

Cain Oil Company owner and retired Michigan State Police officer Charles Cain and his wife Helen, as teacher in the Coleman, Michigan, school system, bought the house in 1948. Here they raised sons John, James and Patrick, and daughter Mary. Cain was also owner of Cain's Mobile Homes Park as well as the gasoline filling station at 1225 North Mission Street. Charles Cain died in 1983 and Helen followed in 1997. The house was purchased in 1994 by accountant and future longtime Mt. Pleasant City Commissioner and Mayor Jon Joslin and his wife Janelle.

622 East Lincoln was built in 1900 by Enos and Mary Crandall. Subsequent owners were: John and Mary Tuoy; John A. Damon; the Daniel Knipe family; and John and Mary Marcus before 1938 when the longest resident owners moved in.

Oil well drilling contractor Michael J. McEvoy and his wife Anna rented the home for a number of years before 1945 purchase. Here they raised daughters Sarah and Jeanne, as well as sons Michael, Edward, Thomas, Robert and Richard. After Michael's death, Anna, a longtime employee of Sacred Heart Church, first as secretary and then as lunch program supervisor, lived here until her 1972 death. Later owners have included: hardware store manager Dean Bice; accountant Robert Elmore; Carol J. Zaremba; and Martin and Rachel McWethy.

625 East Lincoln was built in 1909 by grocer William E. Ratliff and his wife Helen. Subsequent owners have included: Emory and Cynthia Dorn; Art and Violet Savage; Charles and Sarah Durfee; Gordon Drilling Company's Lewis Mc Donald and his wife Dorothy; CMU student activity director Karl E. Metzger and his wife Elaine; contractor Clinton C. Hansen and his hair-stylist wife Norma; geophysicists and oil producers Martin and Olivia Lagina; Roger and Ann Allen, then Bruce Byers with Marsha Biggs.

408 East Maple Note the crosshatched decorative four panel pair of doors on the pyramid roofed "stable turned garage", for this gable front family National Folk home built in 1890 by Civil War veteran George Francisco, *below with grandson Harrison Francisco about 1910.*

George F. Francisco was born in New York, where he enlisted in Company C. 44th New York Infantry early in the Civil War. During the Battle of the Wilderness, in that war, he was wounded in the head and laid with the dead on the battlefield for three days before being picked up by Confederates sorting to retrieve their own. He was placed in the Confederate Libby Prison at Richmond, Virginia. Libby Prison gained an infamous reputation for the overcrowded and harsh conditions under which officer prisoners from the Union Army were kept. Prisoners suffered from disease, malnutrition and a high mortality rate. By 1863, one thousand prisoners were crowded into large open rooms on two floors, with open, barred windows leaving them exposed to weather and temperature extremes.

George Francisco survived the prison, losing an eye and his general health and was hospitalized for years before coming to Mt. Pleasant in 1875, where he married Mrs. Hannah Bowers, who had been a faithful nurse and companion according to his 1913 obituary. The house remained as a rental in the Francisco family, primarily overseen by George's son Harry and later by Harry's son Harrison A. Francisco, who followed his father into the photography studio business at Francisco Photography Studio at 215 West Broadway.

Harrison A. Franciso died in 1990 and the house was sold to Lombard Limited in 1991 and to Paul and Carol Haas in 1994.

511 East Maple The house was built in 1936 by Ray Monroe, an accomplished woodworker. This Cape Cod style house was partially built with lumber from a barn which was torn down on the property. The barn beams are easily visible in the basement of the house. Ray and his wife Olive lived at *519 South Fancher Street.*. The back yards of their property and this Maple St. property are connected.

Built as a rental unit, the house was variously occupied by Mt. Pleasant High School science teacher Gerritt D. Muyskens and his wife Laura; as well as florist Kenneth Harper and his wife Maxine of Harper's Flowers at 305 South Main Street. Maxine and the two girls remained in the Maple Street home until 1961.

In 1961, Monroe rented the house to Monica Pruden of Black, Sivalls & Bryson oilfield tank makers, who eventually bought the property. A variety of owners and renters followed, including Thomas Miller of Central Michigan University and his wife Doris.

In the fall of 2002, the Maple Street house returned to the family when it was purchased by the Monroe's granddaughter and her husband, Dick and Susan Harper Switzer. Dick Switzer operated a barber shop at 616 North Mission for 42 years. The Switzers spent the next nine months restoring the home as much as possible to its original condition. Upon completing the restoration, the home was rented to Sister Andre Kravec of the Sacred Heart Parish.

In the fall of 2010, the home was purchased by Mary Harper, youngest of the Monroe's granddaughters. She continues to live in the house and it is once again "the Harper house".

The Switzers were generous in sharing the story of this home, as well as stories of the Fancher Street houses, *see pages 125 and 126.*

406 East Michigan, ***center, above in a 1919 site photo for the "new" U. S. Post Office building at the southeast corner of Michigan and Normal (University), see page 176.*** The house was built in 1890.

In 1929, it became home to Henry Roethlisberger and his wife Beulah. Henry Roethlisberger, did a variety of things before becoming a respected longtime business man. He was a gas filling station attendant, then worked for Scott's Hardware and Furniture, at the southwest corner of Main and Broadway, *where the 1943 caricature right below was done*, before "hanging out his shingle" as a real estate agent at 106 West Broadway, later moving to 205 East Broadway. Although the Roethlisberger's moved to *612 Anna Street* in the late 1940s, the family retained ownership of this property until 1971. Here they raised son Dale and daughter Trudy. Henry died in 1969 and Beulah followed in 1992.

During the 1953-1976 era, occupants included a succession of renters: shoe salesman Robert Harp and his wife Helen; CMU chemistry professor W, J, Thomas and his wife Margaret; Gould Drug Company pharmacist Richard R. Brandell and his wife Mary Ellen; and CMU teacher Gabriel Y. Chien and his wife Florence. In 1976, the property sold to Edward and Rolaine Franke. From 1983 until 2011, the house was home to Arlene Westhoven, who sold that year to Ryan and Christopher Wallis.

515 East Michigan, also known as 120 South Kinney This address was identified as *120 South Kinney* for many years before the designation changed in recent years to 515 East Michigan. The house was built in 1935 by funeral director George Jay Stinson, who had come to Mt. Pleasant in 1909 and opened a funeral parlor at 116 South Normal Street, now University, before building the present funeral home building at 330 South University in 1940. Stinson had lived caddy-cornered at *203 South Kinney, see page 139* for a number of years before buying this property from attorney Francis H. Dodds and building this house in "Mt. Pleasant brick". Apparently, he liked the basic design so well he nearly duplicated it with the 330 South University Funeral Home.

George Stinson died in 1952 and in 1956, the house was sold to oil producer, Leonard Ward, *left,* of Ward Oil Company, and his wife Ruth A.

Ruth Ward sold the house in 1972 to Isabella County State Bank's Richard R. Bellinger and his wife Mary Alice, here they raised son Scott, longtime editor of the *Michigan Oil & Gas News* magazine.

In 1983, the Bellingers built a new home at 217 South Kinney and sold the house to Mt. Pleasant attorney James S. Fox and his wife Mary Lou, where they raised Jennifer, Stephen, Paul and Sarah.

619 East Michigan A gable front with side wing wood frame structure with an enclosed eaves-level porch and front dual bay windows, this home was built in 1892 by William and Helen Ratliff and sold in 1903 to Thad Ayling, who in turn sold in 1913 to Fred Wilcox.

Cornelius and Mary Brown bought the home in 1919 and sold to Ralph and Nellie Hoot 1920, who in turn sold to John and Adeline Delmater in 1934.

The Delmaters sold the house in 1944 to Belle LaForge and her sister Mable Engfehr. Belle LaForge was the manager of McDonald Hat Shop at 305 East Broadway, which later became Belle's Hat Shop, the only shop devoted exclusively to women's hats ever to operate in Mt. Pleasant.

LaForge sold Belle's Hat Shop in the late 1960s to Lucille Robinson, *see 316 North Main, see page 52*. Belle LaForge died in 1974 and her sister sold the house in 1977 to Mt. Pleasant High School teacher Norman and his wife Anita Hoag, a teacher at both Ganiard and Vowles elementary schools in Mt. Pleasant.

The Hoags sold the property in 1998 to Bridgette H. Bechtold.

113 East Palmer was built in 1927 by legendary auto parts dealer Ben Traines and his wife Rose R. Traines, directly behind Traines Auto Parts store at 802 North Main Street.

Ben Traines was born in 1892 in Riga, Latvia, came to the United States in 1910 and began a fur-buying business in Evart, Michigan. He served in the U.S. Army and moved to Mt. Pleasant upon his return from World War I. In 1924, he bought the inventory of Mt. Pleasant's Transport Truck Company, an early local truck manufacturer, and opened his business at the northeast corner of Main and Palmer in 1925. He built his house right around the corner. The store was to expand four times.

Meanwhile Ben and Rose R. raised three children; Robert, Irwin and Shirley. Active in community activities and charities, he served many years on the Central Michigan Community Hospital Board of Trustees and donated land for the Temple Benjamin synagogue.

Traines died in 1978 and his wife followed in 1982. Members of the Traines family retained ownership of the properties until 1996.

Subsequent owners of the house include George and Marsha Lawrence, as well as Gregory and Carol Hoormann.

Traines Auto and Truck Parts has been closed since the 1990s. The business site, owned by Pickard and Main LLC, is vacant.

221, 310 and 316 East Palmer were all built in the 1890s, probably by Cornelius Bennett whose C. Bennett's Addition was made to Mt. Pleasant in 1882, see *Appendix 1*. More than likely, the homes were built to a uniform pattern by the same builder on speculation to rent or sell at relatively low prices. Many additions to the town were made and populated in that manner after the 1879 arrival of the Pere Marquette train to the depot at 625 North Main Street brought a spurt of north end industrial expansion.

221 East Palmer has been built/owned/occupied by: F. S. Dains 1890; printer Fred McConnell 1926-1941; Jennie Thering 1946-1965; Jim and Jean Dwyer 1965-1981; with renters including *Daily Times-News* Advertising Manager Thomas W. Cradit and Kathy Bard.

310 East Palmer has been owned/occupied by: Honora McHale 1892; fireman Arthur Swan and his wife Alice 1938-1969; renter Leroy D. Hayward, retired, and his wife Pearl 1963-1972; and was owned for a time by Ed Natzel. It was remodeled in 1980.

316 East Palmer has been owned/occupied by: Seneca DeHart 1883; Virgil Gorby, oilfield rig builder and later driller and his wife Mary E. 1946-1978; and Stanley Gillis and his wife Loretta, with children Tim, Terry, Peggy, Nancy and Pat A.

Members of the Gillis family have occupied the house continually since 1978.

519 East Pickard was built in 1905 by James Armstrong and sold in 1908 to Peter H. and Rose Fisher. In 1922, Floyd H. and Bessie Johnson bought the property and sold it in 1923 to Fred and Florence Russell, who in turn sold to Lulu Deeter in 1924. Lulu Deeter held on to the house for awhile before selling in 1938 to Robert Allysworth.

In 1947, the house was sold to Lee Equipment Company, employee Albert Frederick and his wife Audrey. Lee Equipment Company was a farm equipment dealer at 1198 North Mission Street,

The Mt. Pleasant city water tower was built across the street the same year. . The right inset picture above, taken in May of 1947 by Albert of his family on the front steps of their new home: Audrey, Wayne, Joan, Jack, David and Bobby. Summer of 1948, ten year old Bobby, *right in bottom row*, drowned while swimming with friends in an abandoned water filled pit just north of the north terminus of Fancher Street. In the left inset above, Jack Fredrick shows off his motorcycle in 1950 at the west door of the house, outside the kitchen and dining room.

In 1958, the Fredricks sold to Teodor Lytek and his wife Janina, who sold in 1963 to Virginia E Ullery, widow of Richard Ullery. Ullery sold to Liquid Transport and later Johnson Oil Company truck driver Willard K. Gibson Senior. Here they raised Gibson Senior's son W. "Kenny" Gibson, Junior. In 1981, after the 1979 death of his father and 1981 death of Virginia E. Gibson, ownership of the home was transferred to Willard K. Gibson, Junior.

222 East Wisconsin was named as a Centennial Home when the city of Mt. Pleasant celebrated the 100th anniversery of the establishment of the community as a city, the house was built in 1890 by Albert B. Upton and his wife Mell. Albert Upton ran the Hicks, Bennett & Co. Bank in downtown Mt. Pleasant. After he retired, Upton went into the land and lumber business and in 1886 platted the west side of Mt. Pleasant, beyond the Chippewa River, with attorney John C. Leaton for the Leaton Addition to the City of Mt. Pleasant. Later the home was owned by C. W. McClafferty, who sold to James A.Kenny and his wife Clara Kenny died in late 1955 and in 1966 Clara followed.

The house was sold to Director of Nursing at the Mt. Pleasant State Home and Training School, in the northwest corner of Mt. Pleasant at Harris and Pickard Streets, Hazen Pittsley, *right,* and his wife Molly, a nurse.When Pittsley retired in the 1970s, the institution's name had changed to the Mt. Pleasant Regional Center for Developmental Disabilities, to close as the Mt. Pleasant Regional Center in 2009. Originally from Flint, Pittsley worked at Hurley Hospital in Flint.

Harper Hospital in Detroit and Newberry State Hospital before moving to Mt. Pleasant in 1965. He was a hobby beekeeper and owner of Pittsley's Apraries, eventually achieving master beekeeperhood. He also is remembered for a golden voice in singing at masses at Sacred Heart Catholic Church.

Here is where Hazen and Molly raised sons Michael Anthony, Patrick, Mark and Michael Howard.

Hazen Pittsley died in 2001.

301 East Wisconsin, left, built in1894, perhaps by Douglas and Mary Nelson, then sold in 1901 to Gausha and Lydia B. Pennell. Lydia Pennell sold in 1911 to Rufus and Martha Johnson, who later sold to Margaret O'Hara. In 1923, O'Hara sold in the 1950s to oilfield hauler William L. Carney, who rented in the 1960s to Long & Wetzel oilfield worker R. W. Trussell and his wife Katherine, a clerk at the New Yorker clothing store downtown. Carney sold in 1961 to the Sacred Heart Catholic Church, Grand Rapids Diocese, who in turn sold in 1968 to George Seelinger, who sold in 1971 to Marguerite Rice, then bookeeper for the A & P store at 705 East Broadway and later partner in D & M Foodland at the same address. Later owners included: Jack and Elizabeth Denslow; Anthony and Melissa Davis; Mark and Maria Taylor Trust; and Frank Swink and Elizabeth Bennett.

302 East Wisconsin, right, built in1884, probably by Henry S. and Cornelia Benton, the house was sold in 1905 to Henry S. Bouton, whose family owned the property until 1939. In 1939, it was sold to Evaluation Sales & Service Company's Clyde C. Thompson and his wife Henrietta, who owned the property until 1978 when Isabella County Extension's Morley McHalpine and his wife Kathy bought it and rented to Mt. Pleasant Regional Center for Developmental Disabilities Facility Director George Garland. In 1990, the McHalpines sold to Phillip and Ann DeLong, who in turn sold to the Gaynier Ferns Trust in 2003. In 2012, the house was sold to Gene and Teresa Myers.

309 East Wisconsin, above, was built in 1889, probably by Henry W. Wicklein, the property owner in the 1889 to 1901 era. The house was sold in 1901 to Mark Pennells, who in turn sold it to Rufus and Martha Johnson in 1918, who sold to Martha O'Hara in 1924.

From 1925 until 1961, owners of the home were the John B. McCall family. First John B. and his first wife Clara, who died in 1946, then John B. and Olive McCall until John's death in 1952.

Born in 1886, John B. McCall came to Mt. Pleasant from his native Saginaw in 1911 with his brother-in-law, Ernest O. Dexter, *see 401 North Fancher*. McCall and Dexter bought out Ed Smithers at his 201-203 West Broadway location and took over the farm implement and harness business at the location now occupied by the Mt. Pleasant Beauty School. While in the farm implement business, McCall became active in auctioneering and became the leading auctioneer in Isabella County for many years. He and Dexter operated the business until 1935. Along the way, in 1913, McCall became a volunteer with the original Mt. Pleasant Fire Department location at the northwest corner of Michigan and Normal (University) where the horse barns for the horse drawn "steamer" was headquartered. Six years later he became Fire Chief, a post he held for 33 years.

Olive McCall owned the house until 1963 when it was sold to House Hold Appliance, *222 East Broadway*, Secretary-Treasurer Robert A. Wood.

Wood sold in 1968 to Ada and Sandra Duffy. This began a succession of owners including: Margurite Rice; Thelma Simmer; Steve and Lura Way, Jennifer Graney; Joe and Jennifer Denslow and in 2007, Mark and Maria Taylor.

400 East Wisconsin was built in 1891 by William and Nellie Tobin, who sold in 1908 to John and Ella Damon. The Damons sold in 1931 to Rose Marie Hagan (maiden name of Mrs. Robert L. Tope) and in 1938 the property title was transferred to Robert L. and Rose Marie Tope.

Robert L. Tope, *below*, like D. F. Jones of *203 South Kinney,* was a West Virginia oilman who came to central Michigan to pioneer the oil and gas exploration and production industry in Michigan. He was associated with Talbot Oil Company, the Michigan Oil and Gas Company and was involved independently with the oil and gas industry. He was the Chairman of the Picnic Committee for the Michigan Oil And Gas Association Annual Picnic and Reunion the third Thursday of June at the Mt. Pleasant Country Club and was renowned for "picking good weather" for the event. Here the Topes raised daughters Mary Jane and Ruth, as well as sons Donald and Robert. In 1973, Bob sold all his Michigan oil and gas producing properties to his nephew Harry E. Tope, whose H. E. Tope Oil Company prospered following the Arab Oil Embargo in October of that year, which raised oil production per barrel price significantly. Robert L. Tope died in 1974 and Rose Marie followed in 1979.

The property was then sold to Linda Longuski, who paid off the land contract on the property in 1999.

Longuski now owns and operates the Pleasant Dreams Bed and Breakfast establishment at this location

714 East Wisconsin Built in the 1890s by Frederick and Jennie Ruegsegger and his wife Jennie, the house sold in 1920 to Hugh and Elizabeth Watson.

The Watsons sold the house in 1936 to Mt. Pleasant High School teacher Edward J. Grambau, *right*, and his wife Jessie, beginning a 35 year run of Mt. Pleasant High School faculty ownership. The Grambaus raised sons Ray and Roland here.

In 1958, Mt. Pleasant High School (M.P.H.S.) Vocational Director David Reed McGee, Jesser Grambau's brother, *below,* and his wife Elsie, who worked for attorney Allen Lampman, bought the house after seeing their son David graduate with the last class to occupy the M.P.H.S 300 South Fancher Street address. David McGee went on to a successful U. S. Airforce career before returning to Mt. Pleasant after retirement.

In 1971, the McGees sold to Dale and Phyllis Jarrett, owners of the adjacent property to the east facing Mission Street, at 404 South Mission, which has been Jarrett the Jewelers since 1958. A series of renters ensued and in 2005, the house became home to Ambiance Salon and Day Spa, selling the building in 2008 to Vanessa Young Real Estate.

South End
(South of Broadway to Bellows)

South:
Arnold, Douglas, Fancher, Franklin, Kinney, Main, Mission, Oak, Pine, University (Church, Normal, College), and Washington Streets

222 South Arnold Although it appears to front on Illinois Street, this gable front and wing family-style wood frame home, *above in 1929*, carries an Arnold Street address. Built in 1904 by George H. Johnson, who retained ownership until 1930, the home was occupied by George and Kati Stinebower in 1908-1916, as well as Anthony and Mary Schmalzle 1916-1928.

In 1928, Johnson sold to Alonzo and Tara Crapo, who rented the property for two years to Clarence and Hattie Hart, *shown left with a new bus (Hattie is seated in the bus at Clarence's shoulder) in front of their taxi/bus service at 209 West Broadway in the 1930s.* The Harts purchased the house in 1930 and sold in 1942 to Charles R. and Fay R. Woodruff, who rented it to oilfield rigger Harry Wilson and his wife Emma, a telephone operator for Sears Roebuck & Co.

In 1974, the home, *right in 2012*, belonged to Richard Wilson until 1982 sale to Robert Barclay and Margaret L. Brisbane.

710 South Arnold The Tudor Eclectic double gabled shake shingle house was built in 1918 by John MacDonald and his wife Lornita H. In 1920, following John's death, Lornita took ownership and in 1934 sold to Ira P. and Dorothy L. Chase, who in turn sold in 1945 to Elroy Nusbaum. In 1953, Russell Stinson bought the house and sold in 1958 to Harry Helms. Helms sold in 1970 to Bessie Oaks, who sold in 1979 to Alan Schilling and Mary Lou Kreiner.

In 1984, Dorita Davenport bought the property and sold it in 2003 to Michael L. Stemmler. Stemmler sold in 2006 to Jeff Jakeway.

Renters through the years have included: Firestone Manager W. M. Trombley and his wife Ruth; Ferro Stamping Company employee Raymond M. McNamara and his wife Zita; Oak Company product manager Gerald R. Bush and his wife Nancy bookkeeper for McClintic and McClintic.

401 South Arnold This Mansard roof house was built in 1936 by oilman Orrin G. Whitener and his wife Nellie, who sold to accountant Alfred A. Buschle and his wife Margaret in 1939. Later owners include: CMC teacher Ralph L. Witherspoon and his wife Kathleen; auto mechanic Carl Stack and his wife Sylvia; CMU instructor Robert Miller and his wife Gail; Albert Kaufman Jr. and his wife Linda R. and passed to Anne Wilson.

1011 South Arnold, right pre 1984, was built in 1934 by carpenter-painter and later Dow Chemical employee Charles H. Bailey Jr. and his wife Agnes M. who raised Joan A. and Sue A. here. The house remained in the family, with a succession of renter occupants until 1973, when Mt. Pleasant area radio station WCEN personality Bob Banta, later an Isabella County Sheriff's Deputy and now a local photo-historian and his wife Betsy moved in.

From here, we'll let Bob pick up the story:

"We bought the house in 1973 for $13,000, a lot of money back then. In 1984, we doubled the size of the house to about 1,500 square feet by adding a brick portion to the front of the structure. Over the years, sidewalks were added as well as fences along the south property line and the alley. A carport was completed in one day by Amish workmen in 1992. About the same time our 'Bobport' was built, *right,* at the front of the house so I can now sit outside in all kinds of weather to contemplate other jobs I have completed, like cedar shingle work and stain for the house and my collection of local photographs which I've put into scrapbooks for future generations. The finished product is shown right."

805 South Douglas was built in 1917 by Mt. Pleasant Lumber Company co-founder George A. Bugbee and his wife Elizabeth, as a rental. Elizabeth moved here as a widow in 1944 from the big house, *see 802 South Washington,* *see page 210*, where most of their seven children were raised.

Bugbee was from Homer Township of Midland County and worked in Bay City in the lumber industry before returning to Mt. Pleasant to work with W. D. Hood in establishing Mt. Pleasant Lumber Company, which he operated until ill health caused his 1940 retirement and 1943 death. In 1945, the home went to Harzy and Inez Fisher, who sold in 1949 to Dr. Robert F. Hall, who along with running a medical office from the home, raised five children with wife Catherine. In 1972, CMU professor Coleman Levich and his wife Eva bought the house and had it until 1978. The home then became a rental and more than 30 documents have been filed on the house, the latest putting ownership with Dan Schell.

915 South Douglas, below, was built in 1925 by Fred Holstead and his wife Anna, who sold it in 1934 to T. F. and Bessie Caldwell. In 1939, James T. and Mabel Celeste Kennedy bought the house and sold in 1941 to former renter, professional engineer and oil industry associate Herman L. Fruechtenicht, *right,* who would become manager of Michigan Gas Storage, a subsidiary of Consumers Power when they moved on to Jackson MI in 1958. The house then went to oil producer W. R. Swetland and his wife Joan, who sold to retiree Irving Whittemore and his wife Alice in 1967. In 1985, William S. Taylor and Deborah Dahl bought the property, which as a rental has changed hands several times to arrive at the present time under the ownership of 3-Ball Properties.

204 South Fancher was built in 1887 by Mt. Pleasant pioneer businessman, boot and shoe merchant Henry Diittman, *right*, whose name would be spelled Diittman, Dittmann and Dittman over the years in various records.

Born in Germany in 1841, Diittman lost his parents when he was 12 years old and came to the United States at 21 in 1872. He married Margaret Dohm at Grand Rapids, Michigan, and lived in Reed City for eight years, then back to Grand Rapids for two years, gaining knowledge of the footwear business at each stop.

In 1882, he opened on the south side of Broadway in space later to be occupied by shoemaker Alexander Hall. One year later, he opened his store at 133 East Broadway, originally a wooden building. He rebuilt in brick following an 1894 fire and the business would operate at this location with the same name continuously more than ninety years. Here he and Margaret would raise Edward, Helen, M.J., Frank, Bernard. Henry Dittman died in 1922 and Margaret followed in 1925. From 1922 to 1934, the house belonged to son Edward Dittman, *see 320 East Illinois, see page 102*, then went to his sister Helen, where she lived until her 1954 death.

Along the way, the house became a rooming house.

The house was then owned by Oren's Department Store employee Genevieve Theisen from 1954 until her late 1960s death, when the house was then sold to carpenter James Wentworth and his wife Bonnie.

In 1988, Richard Lewis Carey and his wife Bonnie Marie bought the house and then sold to Daniel Meridith Hansen in 1998.

302 South Fancher was the built by Lewis N. Marsh, *left*, of Marsh & Lewis, a mercantile store established in 1879 at the northeast corner of Main and Broadway that the partners purchased in 1889 from founder Frank M. Foster. L. N. Marsh died in 1927. The home was then owned by Mt. Pleasant Postmaster Bert M. Gould and his wife Nellie.

In 1948, Clarence F. Knollenberg, a Sun Oil Company Superintendent, owned the property and home.

The 1950s and 1960s found the house owned and occupied by oilfield trucking and field superintendent for Gordon Oil Company Dean B. Russell, *right,* and his wife Ouita. Years later, in 1978, Russell would be part of a contingent who delivered the first United States built oilfield trucks to China and, since the area where they would be used is similar to Michigan's climate, instructed Chinese oilfield crews in the use and care of those trucks.

George B. Martin and his wife Maxine resided there most of the 1970s.

In 2012, the house is a rental with two apartments and continues to keep its gracious appearance.

409 South Fancher The house was built in 1894 by blacksmith Newton K. Wright. In the 1920s, the house was purchased by Bertram O. Reynolds and his wife Marvel. Reynolds was the owner of the Central Drug Store at 106 East Broadway, “Home of Peninsular Remedies” according to his advertising in the 1926 Mt. Pleasant City Directory.

In the 1930s, the home became one of the many properties of Bessie (Mrs. Ed) Dittman, co-owner of Dittman’s Shoe Store, who lived here for more than a decade.

By the early 1950s, this was the home of United States Department of Agriculture Soil Conservation Service Work Unit Manager John W. Foster and his wife Wilma, a secretary at Mt. Pleasant High School. Here the Fosters raised daughters Patricia and Jeanne.

The Fosters sold to Mt. Pleasant Public Schools teacher Michael C. Smith and his Shepherd Schools teacher wife Jeanne. Here the Smiths raised Paul and Margaret. Later owners included: P.A. Learned; oilman J.W. Neff; Smith (oil) Tools salesman Mike Ramey and his wife. Here the Ramey’s raised Dean, Jeff and Penny.

City of Mt. Pleasant Director of Planning and Community Development Tony Kulik and his wife Kathy, Executive Director of Middle Michigan Development Corporation, bought the home in 1990. Here they raised daughter T. J. Abby.

517-519, above in the 1970s, and 525 South Fancher, at the top of the next page. 519 South Fancher was built in 1900. Consumers Power Manager Ray Monroe and his wife Olive lived at 519 South Fancher Street for more than 60 years. The back yards of their property and the *511 East Maple Street* property, *see page 105,* are connected. The Monroes also owned the house at the NE corner of Fancher, 525 South Fancher.

Since Ray owned both the corner property and the Maple St. property, he built a common driveway and a shared garage between the two houses. The property line goes down the middle of the driveway and through the still existing garage structure.

At some point in the early 1940s, Ray converted the upstairs into a rental unit, which became 517 South Fancher. The first renter of the 517 apartment was Mt. Pleasant High School Coach, and someday superintendent of Mt. Pleasant schools, Carlo Barberi and his wife Kay in the late 1940s.

Other 517 apartment renters included: Central Michigan College Physical Education Instructor William Theunissen and his wife Dorothy in the 1950s; dentist Lawrence Johnson in the late 1950s; Central Michigan University campus barber E. K. Cook and his wife Mary in 1962; followed by Lansing barber Dick Switzer (destined to be Ray and Olive Monroe's grandson-in-law) in 1963; and Embers Restaurant employee Charles E. Howe and his wife Tamara, to name a few. Both the downstairs and upstairs of the corner house at 525 Fancher and the house at 511 E. Maple St. were all rental units.

The house next door to *519* is **525 South Fancher** and was built in 1890 by Thomas J. Winans and his wife Mary. Thomas died in 1898 and his wife Mary lived in the house until her 1934 death. Ray Monroe bought the house from the Winans estate in 1934 and used both upstairs and downstairs as rental units. Early tenants of the upstairs apartment were Ken and Maxine Monroe Harper, Ray and Olive's daughter. The story goes that around 1944, Ray saw his young granddaughter, Susan, playing near an open window in the upstairs apartment and relocated the family to the one story house at *511 East Maple Street.*

Around 1955, Ken relocated to downtown Mt. Pleasant where he owned and operated Harpers Flowers, in a building connected to the home of his parents, Elmer and Edna Harper. The building, together with the house on the corner of Main and Illinois streets, was torn down to make way for the current Verizon building.

Later owners of the Fancher Street properties included: City of Mt. Pleasant policeman Larry G. Kniffen and his wife Mary Lou in 1963; Northeastern Mutual Life Insurance Agent Richard H. Ireland and his wife Patricia in 1963; and, since 1978, Central Michigan University's David I. MacLeod and his wife, a Central Michigan University librarian.

As with *511 East Maple,* the author is grateful to Dick and Susan Harper Switzer for help with this narrative.

606 South Fancher, above in 2012 is salmon colored with a double gable front. The house was built a hundred years ago, in 1912 by Harry Francisco. The Franciscos sold in 1944 to Attorney Edward Lynch, and his wife Dorothy, who held it as a rental until 1976 sale to Buford and Mardie Robinson. In 1979, the Robinsons sold to Michael and Deborah Knoll, who in 1983 sold to Ronald and Donna K. Sheridan who sold in 1984 to oilman Charles S. Fife Jr. Fife sold to Jay and Carol Lanctot in 1986 and in 1989 Gregory and Joan Schmidt brought the real estate relay race to a halt.

The Schmidts made the house, right, an extensive remodeling project, to stand proudly in front of the finished product in 1989.

701 South Fancher has changed very little since 1936 construction by A. J. "Whitey" Weideman, *below*, and his wife Sylvia. Weideman, below, served as the second Executive Secretary of the Michigan Oil And Gas Association, an organization of Michigan oil and natural gas explorers and producers chartered at Mt. Pleasant in 1934. A former oilfield drilling contractor and producer, "Whitey" had served two terms in the Michigan Legislature before accepting the Association Chief of Staff in 1938, serving until ill health caused his March, 1941 resignation. During his tenure, the efforts of many in the industry were rewarded with the passage of Act 61 of 1939, Michigan's Oil and Gas Law, which, with "tweaks" from 1939 passage to the present continues to be considered classic oil and gas regulation.

In 1940, the Weidemans sold the Tudor Revival/Storybook-style home to Floyd A.M. Taylor, a Sunoco Oil distributor headquartered in the Taylor Building at the northeast corner of Broadway and Franklin streets in downtown Mt. Pleasant. Floyd died in 1961 but his wife Ethel continued living in the house until the house was sold in 1963 to Mt. Pleasant attorney Loren Gray.

Loren and successive generations of the Gray family have sequentially called the house home to the present.

701 South Fancher This front gable Folk style home with gabled dormer was built in 1924 by Samuel N. Lirones and his wife Flossie Gertrude Schust Holitbaugh Lirones.

Samuel Lirones was born in 1892 in Kahazea, Tripoli, the son of Kristoula and Nicolas Lirones, who emigrated to the United States when he was a child.

Sam served in the United States Army during World War I and was a an active member of the Veterans of Foreign Wars, American Legion and the Polar Bears.

He married Gertrude in 1920 at Big Rapids and in 1923 moved to Mt. Pleasant, where he was in the shoe repair and hat cleaning business at 307 East Broadway for many years.

Here Sam and Gertrude Lirones raised Loren, Lujean, David, Ralph, Elodie, Daniel, Keith and Samuel.

Gertrude died in 1961 and Sam remarried Markia Roumelratou in Athens, Greece, a year later.

Sam died in this home in September, 1979, after a long illness

711 South Fancher A reproduction of the original art rendering of this home by Mt. Pleasant artist David Ellis appears on the cover of this book.

Alexander Hall, a boot and shoe maker from Montgomery County, New York, came to the Mt. Pleasant area in 1874 and opened a shop. In 1877, he bought 40 acres of land in Section 15, Union Township, Isabella County, adjacent to the town, which, after platting 20 acres, he annexed to the town in 1878. Hall retained a five acre wooded plot for himself, where he built a house. Hall's house burned in 1913.

This French-chateau-style residence was built in 1935 by Reno Ter Veen on the site of the former Hall's Woods for William Edward Harris, of Harris Milling Company. Harris Mill, a feed and flour mill on West Broadway, used the power generators driving their mill from waterpower provided by the dammed Chippewa River, to provide early Mt. Pleasant with electricity.

In 1944, the Harris family sold the property to oil producer/refiner J. Walter Leonard of Leonard Refineries, who occupied it until 1977, when it was purchased by Ralph J. "Bud" and Mary Ann Fisher in 1977.

The house has four fireplaces, five separate "living quarter" units of bedroom and private bath. The Fishers modernized the kitchen from shiny steel cupboards and a dumbwaiter, finding that arrangement not workable, but left the structure intact, except for occasional changes in wallpaper.

The home was included on the Mt. Pleasant Area Historical Society Christmas House Walk in 1992.

1002 South Fancher This Georgian Colonial style home with a single door Ogee design front entry was built in 1936 by building contractor J. Lloyd and Marion M. Cole who lived there with sons Steven and Robert. J. Lloyd Cole was the sone of prominent builder Lewis G. Cole, *see 701 South University, page 191.*

In 1947, the home was sold to Gordon Oil Company President I. W. "Bucky" Hartman, *left,* and his wife Velma. Hartman was an accountant who came to Mt. Pleasant with Gordon from Bremen, Ohio, in the 1930s. In 1943, he was elected president of that company following the death of Howard Atha, the company's first president, in 1943. During World War II, he served on the Petroleum Administration for War (PAW) District 2 Production Committee. Hartman would be Mayor of Mt. Pleasant in 1949 and eleventh President of the Michigan Oil And Gas Association in 1951, seventeen years after his boss at Gordon Oil, Howard Atha, was elected the first President of the Association.

Here I. W. and Velma Hartman would raise son John and daughter Susan.

In the 1970s, the Hartmans donated the home to Central Michigan University and in 2000 the University sold the home to Gordon and Shindorf A. Risbrider, who in turn sold it in 2011 to Stephen and Heather Knewston.`

420 South Franklin Renowned physician, surgeon and civic leader Dr. Charles D. Pullen, *below* in 1906, and his wife Clara built the gambrel-roof Georgian Colonial home in 1908 on land they bought from Peter Richards.

Pullen, for whom Mt. Pleasant's Pullen Elementary School would be named in the 1950s, was born in 1864 at Allegan, Michigan. Dr. Pullen came to Mt. Pleasant following graduation with a Medical Degree from University of Michigan in 1892. He continued honing his professional skills with post-graduate courses in Chicago and New York, while expanding his Mt. Pleasant practice. He was physician for the Mt. Pleasant Indian Industrial Schools for ten years, serving on the Mt. Pleasant Board of Education for five years and was a captain in the U.S. Army during World War I. Pullen was elected to the 1935 Michigan legislature. Dr. Pullen died in 1940, survived by his wife, Clara, son Dwight French Pullen and daughter Marian Clarice Pullen Pepper.

Later occupant owners of the house included optometrist George Foland in 1940 and optometrist George L. Brown in 1955, both of whom had practices at 125 East Broadway. In the 1970s, the home was owned by Assistant Central Michigan University professor Leo Kipfmeuller and his wife Patricia.

510 South Franklin - This carefully preserved right side winged modified Gothic Revival home with board and batten peaks and a single story porch is painted in pastels, dominantly blue, in Victorian era fashion. This type is found scattered among areas of the north settled in the 1880s. The house was built in 1888 by Delos and Whay Ervans, who sold in 1912 to Margaret and Angela McCarthy, who in turn sold to William J. Quinlan and his wife Barbara in 1926, who in turn sold to Chauncy Mead in 1931.

In 1937, ownership of the property went to sons Frank A. and Clarence Mead, who sold to Charles and Sarah Quinlan.

In 1938, the house sold to shoe repairman Leonard Roberts and his wife Lillian, who sold to crude oil dispatcher Elwood Kisby and his wife Ann, who in turn sold in 1953 to McClure Oil Company's Fred Heinlein and his wife Mildred. Here they raised daughter Joyce Ann and for awhile in the 1970s rented the homes apartment to Lynch, Gallagher, Lynch and Kerr secretary Joyce Urquhart.

Fred Heinlein died in 1971 and Mildred Heinlein sold the house in 1979 to former McDonald's House of Cabinets owner Joseph McDonald and his wife Jennifer, who with loving care continue to maintain the home in picture postcard condition, fronted with an ornate picket fence.

The house was designated a Centennial site when the City of Mt. Pleasant celebrated the 100th Anniversary of its 1889 designation as a city.

612 and 612 ½ South Franklin This tree-shadowed Georgian Colonial home with a hipped roof, along with one story bay windows on both the south side and east front facing was built in 1890 according to City of Mt. Pleasant Assessment records. This would have been during the period of ownership by George Mc Donald.

Eugene Charles and Clara Jane Nardin bought the house in 1900 and sold in 1925 to Stirling and Alex Hursh, who in turn sold it to concrete contractor James Bent and his wife Bessie.

In 1951, carpenter Harold Robert Verleger and wife Mildred Gloria, sometimes called Millie in the records, a teacher who taught at Riverdale and Alma schools during the years. Harold Verleger was later the developer of the Southgate Subdivision, a 1959 addition to Mt. Pleasant, and Southgate 2, an expansion added to the city in 1961. Here the Verlegers raised sons Robert and Richard also known as "Rick".

The property is now under the ownership of the Mildred G. Verleger Trust.

612 ½ South Franklin Through the years, renter occupants of this address have included: Broadway Bar, 201 West Broadway, owner Cyril La Pointe and his wife Mae in the 1950s; State Police officer Kenneth Battey and his wife Charlene in the 1960s; and a brigade of college students varying with the school years.

614 South Franklin in 1906 finds the extended family of Lee J. and Mary E. Doud in front of Lee and May's newly acquired home. *Front row, l. to r.:* Charlie Everest, Henrietta Tygart's brother; Alice Lulu Tygart; Ida Tygart; Tom Tygart, a Civil War veteran; and Henrietta Everest Tygart. *Back row,* left to right are: Lee Doud; May Tygart-Doud with baby Darl; Ray Doud; Bernie Doud; Helen Doud; Helen Matie Tygardt, and Tom and Charlie Tygart

The house was built in 1899 by David Rodman and sold to Lee and Mary Doud in 1906. Ten years later the house was bought by Chester W. Riches and his wife Nell. Chester was a teller with Exchange Savings Bank and would ascend to it's presidency by 1953. In 1958, the house was occupied by Central Michigan College Reserve Office Training Corps officer Abraham Lincoln, who bought it in 1959. Lincoln sold to George D. Noch, a teacher at Mt. Pleasant High School, and his wife Jeannette. in 1974. The Nochs sold in 1977 to Bruce Schaefer and his wife Carole, owners of Schaefer's Mens Wear at 2200 South Mission. In 1985, Schafer sold the home to James Dennis, a salesman in his clothing store, who continues to own the home, *right*, in modern times.

1019 South Franklin was built in 1904 by Franklin and Mary Ellis, who had bought the property from Charles A. and Etta H. Moody.

Central Michigan State Teachers College engineers Emil T. and Maud E. Oberg bought the house in 1925, continued the residence tradition of renting part of the house and an apartment over the garage in back.

In 1933, renters included, right to left Wes Duno, Floyd Northcutt, Loyd Northshine and Myron "Mike" Georgia.

In 1955, the house became a Delta Omicron Tau Kappa Epsilon chapter, who eliminated use of the garage to house automobiles and remodeled to make the ground floor of the structure into residence rooms, and in 1961 the Oberg estate sold to Eleanor Nicks. In 1973, Delta Omicron sold to Consolidated Apartments and in 1977 American Security Bank sold it to Robert and Lillian Byron. The Byrons sold in 1981 to Jeremy L. Jones who sold to Doris and Charles Sherwood in 1985.The Sherwoods assigned the property to Rentwood Management in 2000. .

116 South Kinney, right in background. In the 1985 photograph *above,* Melanie (McClain) Allan gets ready to move into an apartment at *117 South Kinney*, while her mother Joyce McClain, sister Beth Ann (McClain) Nesbitt, and Beth Ann's son Jamie Wernette pose while helping with the move.

Behind them across the street, is the white frame house at *116 South Kinney*, built in 1919 by Howard E. and Minnie Chatterton. In 1930, the Chatterons sold the house to Farmers Grain proprietor Glenn Knapp and his wife Flossie. Glenn died in the 1950s and Flossie followed in 1961, after which the home became the property of Harold B. and Ethel Knapp. The Knapp era for the house ended in 1965, when it was sold to Esther Yunker, then in 1973 to Richard and Esther Wheeler and in 1976 to Betty Wilson.

Raymond and Mary Whalen bought the house in 1979 and sold in 1985 to geophysicist Claude Woods, *right,* and his wife Betty. In 1989, the Woods sold to Shepherd's Carl and Rita Eisenberger.

Renters of the house, and 116 ½ , the apartment therein, have included: Ferro Stamping die maker Jack E. Bemis; CMU teacher Charles Bett and his wife Gloria; Jean Ingersoll; Roscoe P. Martin and His wife Dorothy; CMU graduate student Richard Kuchniki; Mrs. Richard Wheeler; and, ironically, in 2012, a grownup Jamie Wernette *right above*, at 10 years old in 1985.

202 South Kinney The house was built around 1900, under the ownership of Dudley A. Pease. In the early 1920s, dry cleaner Charles J. Warner and his wife Lottie bought the property and began to "really clean up" opening the College Cleaners, which boasted this address but faced Michigan Street at the alley between Fancher and Kinney streets behind the house, *shown below in 2012.* Here on South Kinney they raised Charles Junior, Ronald and Durward.

By the late 1930s, Warner's dry cleaning holdings had grown to include, besides College Cleaners: American Dry Cleaners and Dye Works – 219 South Main; Broadway (O'Connors) Cleaners - 115 East Broadway; and Nu Way Cleaners – 106 Court Street. Charles J. Warner, Senior, died in 1968 and his wife followed in 1972.

The house then sold to retired Mt. Pleasant High School teacher Forrest Williams and his wife Bernice, who also rented a portion of the house to Mark and Patricia Zingery children Lynette Ann and Mathew Mark.

Later owners include: Gail P. Scukaner; Daisaku and Yumiko Yamamoto; and Aparna Lhila.

203 South Kinney Built in 1904 by George and Ellen Hicks, this modified Colonial wood framed home with a center gable and central chimney was sold by Ellen Hicks to Nellie Gilpin in 1913, who sold in 1914 to George Jay and Mary Louise Stinson, see *515 East Michigan, see page 107*, who sold in 1935 to Dennis F. Jones, *below*, and wife Hattye Bell.

A former school teacher from Roane County, West Virginia, Jones came to Mt. Pleasant in 1929 in the infancy of Mt. Pleasants oil boom in the aftermath of the 1928 discovery of the Mt. Pleasant oilfield at the Midland/Isabella County line. As the industry expanded, D. F. Jones was at the vanguard of the state's oil and gas development, participating in all aspects of the oil business including development of the Six Lakes natural gas field, which ultimately was converted to one of the state's largest natural gas storage fields. Jones was also one of the first members of the Michigan Oil And Gas Association when chartered in Mt. Pleasant in 1934. He was an independent operator and continued leasing until just a month before his 1975 death at 85 years old shortly after the Jones celebrated their 60th wedding anniversary. D.F. and Hattye B. Jones had three daughters: Freda, Olga (Denison) and Virginia. Virginia preceded D. F. in death and Hattye B. Jones died in 1996 at 102 years of age. In 1978, the house sold to Mt. Pleasant City police officer, later detective, Howard Sageman and his wife Karen, along with children Lori, John, Melissa, and Jennifer.

205 South Kinney This classic Craftsman style home with a side gabled roof and wide expanse enclosed front porch and front dormer was built in 1920 by A. Henry and Minnie Bailey, who sold in 1938 to George Pfetsch, and his wife Gertrude Alice, children Robert and Eleanor. The Pfetsch family also rented to salesman Howard Crawford and State Inspector John B. McLain and his wife Louise.

Ownership was transferred in 1967 to Robert Pfetsch and Eleanor Pfetsch Young , who sold in 1973 to Bernard F. and Clara Sanderson and their daughter Mary Alice Bellinger, *see 515 East Michigan , page 107 along with 213 and 221 North Kinney, page 40.*

In 1988, ownership was recorded to Richard and Mary Alice Bellinger, who in 1993 completed sale of the property to their son *Michigan Oil and Gas News* magazine editor Scott Bellinger, *right*, and his wife Central Michigan University English Department instructor Lori S. Rogers-Bellinger.

216 South Kinney, shown in 1985 Built in 1905 on Lot 5, Block 21 of the Kinney Addition to Mt. Pleasant by William Ritchie, whose widow Marie sold it to William and Theresa Bennett in 1911. The house sold to Edith Hawksworth in 1913. The Hawksworth's would own the place until 1947, when Edith's estate took bids and sold to Arnold and Helen Koch, both employed by Mt. Pleasant High School, next door, he as a science teacher and she in the cafeteria. The Kochs raised sons: David, James and Peter there and sold to Jim and Sally Wojciechowski in 1984.

Pleased with their "nice old house", the Wojciechowskis later received the following letter from the previous owners letting them know how the "nice old house" got that way.

September 25, 1985

Dear Friends:

For a long time I have had the idea that I would write you to give some information about your house which I thought might be of interest to you. But I am one of the world's great procrastinators. Your kindness in sending the picture by way of our good friend, Helen Johnson seemed to give me the push I needed. We are glad to know that you are enjoying the house. We were pleased to live there for 37 years despite some deficiencies. You might like to have the old deeds which I am enclosing. I assume that the 1900 deed is for the lot only. By 1905 there was probably a structure. It no doubt consisted of only the two north rooms. The old roof can be seen from the front attic. I have no idea when the other parts were built, probably in two or three stages.

In 1947 we were desperately in need of a place to live. Mt. Pleasant was in the middle of an "oil boom" and there had been little building during World War II.

We learned of the Hawksworth estate two days before the deadline for submitting bids. The administrator and the house keys were in Grand Rapids. So we walked around the house, looked in the windows, and submitted a bid which was accepted. When we got inside, we were dismayed. I spent night after night until one or two in the morning with a steamer removing 5 or 6 layers of wall paper. That uncovered the old sand plaster which needed endless patching before being covered with texturing material. The floors needed sanding and patching.

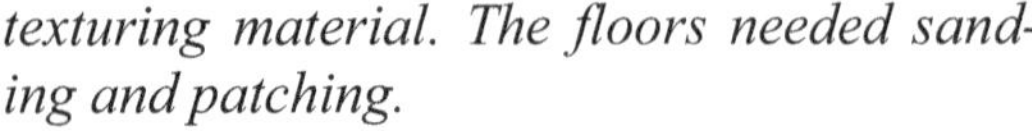

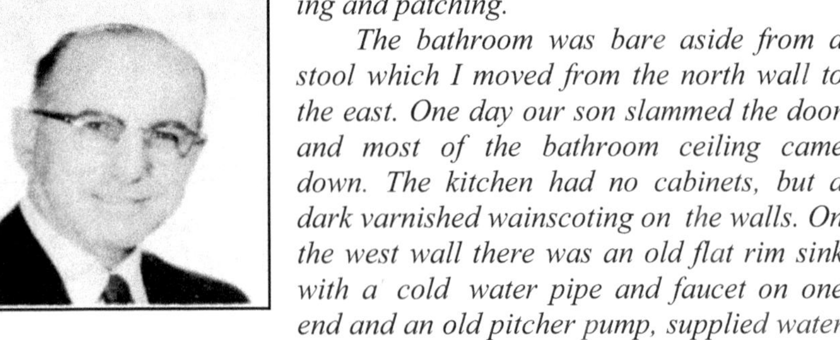

The bathroom was bare aside from a stool which I moved from the north wall to the east. One day our son slammed the door and most of the bathroom ceiling came down. The kitchen had no cabinets, but a dark varnished wainscoting on the walls. On the west wall there was an old flat rim sink with a cold water pipe and faucet on one end and an old pitcher pump, supplied water from the cistern, on the other. On the east wall there had been a combination gas-wood range. The smoke pipe had been. routed through the wall into the dining room, then through the ceiling into the bedroom, and into the attic where it entered a short chimney.

The cellar had a dirt floor and the ceiling too low for even a short person to stand straight. My son and I dug out a lot of sand and poured a floor. The furnace vent went through the ceiling into the southeast corner of the second living room and up through that ceiling into the northwest bedroom where it entered a brick chimney which was supported by a heavy wooden bookcase. After I built the chimney on the north side of the house and moved the bookcase to the rear attic.

I never met Wilbur Hawksworth. Before my time at the school he was an employee of Mt. Pleasant High School, which stood just to the south where the Sacred Heart Catholic Church and Administration Building is now. I think he operated the coal-fired boilers and brought over a lot of cinders for the driveway, some of which may still be in evidence. He was also a truck gardener. On the southwest corner of the lot, he had a two-story barn with a basement which could be heated for storing vegetables. I think he had horses at one time. When we bought the property the fuse box was in the barn. There were two circuits; one for the barn and one for the house. At that time we had an "ice box". There was an ice plant at the corner of Kinney and Pickard. I am enclosing one of Hawksworth's land contracts which relates to his purchase of one of the garden plots. At that time there were open fields on the west part of the city. In fact there were only about three houses south of High Street and west of the railroad.

When we came, there was a house to the south between us and Illinois. It belonged to the school and was used for music classes, etc.. When the new high school was built in 1957, the house was torn down and the area converted for physical education. That required the closing of that block of Wisconsin Street. When the church was built, the space became a parking lot, as you know. One winter, while we were in Florida the plows pushed the snow against the fence. That is why the fence is so crooked..

Helen Johnson wrote that you were putting new wall covering on the hall and stairway.. We did the job the last time but it is still. hard for me to believe it. We tried to use "permanent" material because we never expected to repeat it. I can't tell you how we did it except that we had stepladders, straight ladders and planks. I also built the kitchen cabinets, did most of the plumbing, and installed most of the insulation. I had professional help with the wiring.

I think I ran out of energy as old age caught up with me. We spent most winters after 1968 out of Michigan. We are sure the old house is in good hands and we wish you much happiness during your stay in it.

Sincerely,
Helen and Arnold Koch

216 South Kinney in 2012

303 South Kinney was built in 1906 by Kirby and Alvina Westfall. The Westfalls sold the house in 1915 to attorney Joseph Schnitzler and his wife Kathryn, who sold it in 1951 to accountant George R. "Rollie" Denison and his wife Olga. G. R. Denison worked for Gordon Oil Company and later, with partner Dean Eckersley, formed the oilfield Service Company Lease Management, Inc., still operating in 2012 under the ownership of Jack R. Harkins and Rudy Kler. In 1978, the house was sold to Central Michigan University Psychology Department Chair William F. Hawkins and his wife Doris. In 2010, the home went to David and Danae Petrella, who in turn sold it to Christopher W. Cataldo in 2012.

407 South Kinney has obviously been remodeled since initial 1879 contruction by John Gorman. From the 1930s until the mid-1950s, the house belonged to Harris Milling Company's Robert V. Harris. Harris sold to Isabella County Drain Commissioner and insurance man L. D. Richmond and his wife Marie. Here they raised sons Donald M., Thomas F., Allen J. and William L, along with daughters Mary E., Ann M., Alice J. and Linda D. L. D. Richmond died in 1973, and Marie sold the house in 2001 to Timothy and Mary Ann O'Neil.

415 South Kinney was built in 1914 by electrician John P. Murphy and stayed in the Murphy family with teacher Katherine Murphy in the 1930s and teacher Miss Agnes Murphy until the early 1960s and 1970s. Following Agnes Murphy's 1975 death, the house was sold to clothier University Shop owner Charles J. Fitzpatrick, now Director of Central Michigan University's LaBelle Entrepreneurial Center, and his bookkeeper wife Nancy. In 2010, the Fitzpatricks sold the house to Katherine J. Ballinger.

424 South Kinney Built in 1910 by Ransalaer Whitney and has variously been the home of: Howard G. and Florence N. McMacken, who raised present-day Gratiot County historian David McMacken there in the 1940s; oilfield driller Leroy A. Lovell and his wife, Virginia a switchboard operator at Central Michigan Community Hospital; Mt. Pleasant Supply's Jeffrey Heintz and Fortino Beverage Company salesman Michael Heintz in the 1970s and 1980s. In 1997, Barbara Livernois et al sold the house to Dallas Kelsey III.

715 South Kinney This Tudor Revival style house was built in 1920 in a contour that suggests it was built as an apartment house. The style, fashionable in the 1920s, is loosely based on medieval prototypes, often with false or ornamental external beams with stucco or masonry veneer and steeply pitched roofs. Sixteen years later, the address became a near neighbor of the track and athletic field, part of the Fancher Elementary School, just south across High Street.

Longest extensive residents of the house were William and Katherine Rankin, probably the people who had the house built. They resided there until 1946.

Other residents over the years have included: attorney Russell L. Furbee and his wife Maud; Central Student Justin Young; teacher Henrietta Kaminske; an R. C. Altrogge; a C. A. Carnahan; a Mrs. Mae MacDonell; and long term resident Mrs. Mable Jones.

In 1946, ownership of the property went to real estate broker Ralph D. Crapo and his wife Margaret. In the 1963 Mt. Pleasant City Directory, an O.C. Miller is listed as owner of the property along with owners the aforementioned Crapo and Mrs. Jones. Continually occupied by renters, the house was owned in 1978 by Clifford Theisen and had three resident renters in 1978.

Now called "The Alamo" apartments, current ownership resides with Ronald and Theresa Osbourne of New Baltimore, Michigan, according to the City of Mt. Pleasant Assessment website.

936 South Kinney was built in 1936 by insurance agent Arlie C. Osborn and his wife Catherine. Here they raised son Jack and daughter Carolyn. Arlie Osborn died in 1984 and Caroline followed in 2001. In 2000, Catherine Osborn sold the house to Cynthia Devers and Lisa Boyd, who in turn sold in 2002 to Michael and Debra Martin.

1009 South Kinney In 1941, C. L. McGuire, Inc. Vice President Allan E. Morrow and his wife Bernice built this home that features a "drive through" garage to the alley behind. Allan Morrow would go on to become Vice President of Leonard Refineries, President of the Michigan Oil And Gas Association and Chairman of the Board of Isabella Bank & Trust. Here, he and Bernice raised daughters Martha E. and Sue B.

In 1999, the house sold to Sacred Heart Catholic Church and has been used as the rectors home since that time

430 South Lansing right This house was built in 1904 by Maggie Garvin on land owned in 1900 by the Church of Christ. It was bought in the 1920s by Mrs. Blanche Strange, who shared the house with roomers in 1939 for instance with secretary Lois Robinson and teacher Ruth Pobanz. In 1947, the house sold to Eldorado Company Superintendent Frank A. Schrot and his wife Margaret. Oilman Paul Mongeau and his wife Lorena, a secretary for CMU, called the house home in the 1960s. Margaret A. Tanner, Beard Oil bookkeeper, bought the house in the late 1960s and in 2011, the Maxine Tanner Trust sold it to Andrew and Catherine Williams.

508 South Lansing, left, built in 1904 by Howard and Carrie James, the house sold in 1908 to Miles Welch and his wife Mary. Mary Welch died in 1920 and Miles died in 1924, after selling in 1923 to automobile salesman John T. Carey and his wife Bernice. John T. Carey was a lifelong Mt. Pleasant resident and an active member of the Moose Lodge and the Mt. Pleasant Knights of Columbus Council 1297. Here John and Bernice raised John and daughter Frances. John died in 1972 and Bernice, after assigning the home to daughter Frances and her husband Charles Reihl in 1984, died here in 1986. In 1987, the Carey's granddaughter Sharon and her husband William Brown bought the home and lived there before selling to Kenneth and Janel Hisey. In 2012, City of Mt. Pleasant Assessment records show Stephen H. and Kelly Johnson as owners.

600 South Lansing, also known as 314 East Walnut This brick red entry-gabled Craftsman home has two faces. Built in 1926 by druggist Mynard E. Butts and his wife Mary Josephine, the Butts raised son Mynard Butts, Junior here. The Butts Drug Store was located at 110 South Main Street occupied by First Bank offices in modern times. In the late 1940s, Mynard Butts, Jr. and his wife Rose lived over the drug store at 110 ½ South Main with children Mynard Butts III and Bonnie.

The house got its "second face", *below*, in 1953, when the Butts sold to Daniel and Melva Coyne. Dan was a distributor for Standard Oil Company through Coyne Oil Company, with offices at his home. Dan used the north side wing of the house as an office and to keep customers from coming to the front door of the house facing Lansing, where he would have to direct them around to the side of the house, he listed his office address as 314 East Walnut so clients would come to the Walnut Street door.

The Coynes sold the house to Mt. Pleasant Junior High School teacher Thomas C. Lyman and his wife Mary in 1963, who in turn sold it in 1965 to Central Michigan University professor Albert P. Resetar and his wife Jane, who lived there with son Mike Resetar.

In 1979, the Resetars sold to Michael and Jane Kwiatkowski, who in turn sold to Charles and Onlee Bowdon.

Michael and Patricia Gostola bought the home in 1993.

617 South Lansing, left This home was built in 1902 by Joseph and Eugenia Bronstetter, assigned in 1937 to Mary Bronstetter. In 1939, oilfield worker Lawrence G. Higginbotham, his wife Irene and daughter Joan called this address home.

In 1948, Mt. Pleasant High School teacher John W. Wiley and his wife Ella bought the house. John Wiley would later become Principal of the Mt. Pleasant Junior High School at 301 South Fancher in 1958, and when the South Fancher location was abandoned in 1972 , would be Principal of Mt. Pleasant's West Intermediate School at 4400 South Bradley on Mt. Pleasant's west side.

Here the Wileys raised Jack E., Jerry R., Dick B. David D., and Donald J. which may explain why, for a while, the Wileys were local representatives for World Book Encylopedias. In 1993, the property was assigned to the John and Ella Wiley Trust, which sold in 2002 to Michael T. Mansfield.

624 South Lansing, right Built in 1910 by Charles and Ida Rogers, the house passed through several owners before coming under the ownership of Michigan Consolidated Gas Company employee Albert Barnhart and his wife Ivah in the 1930s. Here they raised Vera, Rita, Iva and Eugene. Albert Barnhart died in 1957 and Ivah continued living there until the early 1970s, when the house was sold to Larry Sommers, who sold to John and Deborah Brocavich in 1989, who sold to MHC Properties in 1995 and the house became a rental with ownership through Craig and Marsha Zeneberg, KT Investments and finally Adam and Allison Kieft.

304 South Main was built in 1879 by Samuel Templeton and sold in 1897 to Dr. Albert T. Getchell, *left*, and his wife Ella, *above in front of the home*. Getchell maintained both home and offices here before selling in 1911 to move to *514 South Main Street*, see page 155.

Through the years, the structure has served as offices for Dr. Lionel Davis and home for he and wife Lucille in the 1930s and 1940s. Primarily though, in more recent times it has been an apartment house for such as: in 1940 - Columbia Oil and Gas owner George W. Scheid and his wife Marie, along with Voorhees Drilling Company's Virgil M. Voorhees; and 1948 – accountant Frank Renner and Robert E, Jones with his wife Mabel. Owned by Mrs. Milan Crapo in the 1950s and 1960s, renters included: oil producer William Mesel; retired Porter West;and Lee Lawrence. In the 1970s, it was home to: oil producer Alan S. Gray and his wife Grace; Raymond McNamara's widow Zida; CMU professor Norman Rasulis and his wife Dola; and student Gloria Peavey.

Right in 2012, the house was remodeled in 1953. Insurance man Robert Acker bought the house in 2000 and in 2006 his estate sold to Family Properties LLC.

405 South Main This brick Queen Anne style home was built in 1880 by Langton and Pamela M. Bently, who bought the property from the Albert Fox estate. Mary Ann Lance bought the house in 1883 and sold it to Lydia Kaup in 1899, who owned it for 10 years, selling to Charles W. Campbell in 1909. Charles W. Campbell was builder of the five story Campbell Building at 107 South Main. Here he and wife Sophornia raised Effie and Willard. Campbell died in 1928 and the next year the house sold to Vern V, Moulton, who held ownership until 1947.

Dr. Howard R. Woodruff bought the home in 1947 and converted a portion of the ground floor to an office for his practice of dentistry for the next several decades. Howard Riley Woodruff was a graduate of Central Michigan Normal School and the University of Michigan Dental College. He played clarinet and saxophone for dance bands while attending Central and taught music in Detroit, while practicing dentistry there, before coming to Mt. Pleasant in 1936.

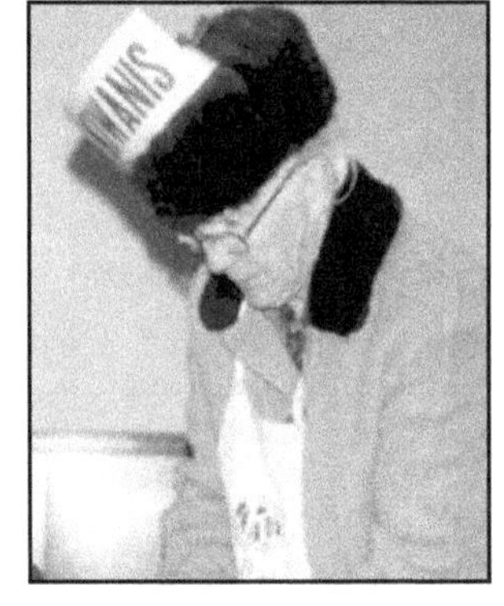

He was a World War II veteran and a Bronze Star recipient. He also was a 50 year member of Kiwanis, where he is shown, *right*, during an Annual Old Newsboys Christmas Newspaper sale.

Here he and his wife Evelyn raised sons Thomas and William, along with daughter Nancy. Evelyn died in 1982 and Howard followed in 1986.

412 South Main This Arts and Crafts Bungalow Kit House was fasionable in the pre-World War I era of expanding prosperity, when many people who had lived in apartments were able to buy homes for the first time. This type of home was fashioned after traditional homes in India, with overhanging roofs, simple porches and bands of windows.

Built sometime around 1900s by Lewis E. Royal, who owned the property from 1888. The house was sold in 1920 to salesman Russell Collin and his wife Mae. The Collin family would own the home until the mid-1960s but Mae Collin, now owner, would move to the apartment over the garage, *412 ½ South Main, right above*, and rent the main house to Central Michigan College Public Relations director Gilbert O. Maienknecht and his wife in the early 1950s, then to Central Michigan University Military Science Instructor William C. Jones and his wife Tina in the 1960s.

In 1965, the house sold to Dow Chemical employee William C. Hall and his wife Bonita, an employee of Ferro Stamping Compay. In 1980, the house was sold to the Sigma Phi Housing Corporation. The house sold to Drew and Leah Dysinger in 1991 and again in 1993 to Harold Shoemaker. Stefanich Management became the owner in 2003 and in 2005 Kevin and Beth Gibbons assigned the property to KBG Properties.

Other renter occupants of 412 ½ South Main over the years included Hycalog diamond drilling engineer John M Brewer and his wife Patricia L., an office worker at Central Michigan Community Hospital as well as Central Michigan University students Randy Bell and Ronald Kramer.

420 South Main was built in 1884 by lawyer Lewis E. and Laura Royal. Lewis E. Royal studied law at Michigan State University and was admitted to the bar in 1896. Lewis served as Mayor of Mt. Pleasant in 1889 and, after Mary and Lester graduated Mt. Pleasant High School in 1902, the Lewis family sold the house to Arthur N. and Florence Ward.

In 1914, the Wards sold to Jacob, Ruth and Walter Neff, who sold to Peter and Anna Mary Gruss, who in turn sold in 1924 to Mae Keeler, who sold in 1926 to teacher Ernest J. Merrill and his wife Pearl.

The 1930 widowed Mrs. William D. Hood bought the home in 1931. William D. Hood was owner of the Hood Lumber Company. Mrs. Alvira Hood would own the home until her 1953 death, when the house was sold to Mt. Pleasant oil and gas attorney Ray Markel , *below*, who moved to southwestern Michigan following the discovery of the Scipio quadrant of the Albion-Scipio oilfield by his chief clients K. P. Wood and Tom Mask. Markel sold the home to Robert M. Klein, owner of Klein's Wallpaper, Paint and Home Improvement at 214 East Broadway, and his CMU teacher wife Helen P. Here the Kleins raised Pattie, Sally, Randa, Arnold and Mark.

Richard G. Reava , Director of Education at the Mt. Pleasant State Home and later a partner in Reava Sewing Center, along with his wife Joyce bought the house in 1971 and lived here with children Doug, Chip and Jeff until 1991 when they sold to Lawrence and Angela Brandon. The Brandons sold in 1997 to Richard J. and Carrie Isarelli, who sold in 1998 to Pat and Marsha Funnell.

In 2006, David and Cindi Verwey bought the house.

514 South Main was the first house in Mt. Pleasant built to a set of blueprints. The Queen Anne style built in 1879 by attorney Michael Devereaux, *left,* who served as Mayor of Mt. Pleasant in 1890-91 and again in 1907. Devereaux's family moved to Michigan the year of his birth in upstate New York to settle on a Livingston County farm. Devereaux attended regular schools until he was 18, then a private seminary in Howell, Michigan, followed by the start of a venture into school teaching. He taught in Osceola Township, as well as in Howell in Livingston County, and then was placed in charge of a school at the village of Zilwaukee in Saginaw County. He later expanded his education with two years at the State Normal School at Ypsilanti then spent five years as principal of the Ontonagon, Michigan, schools. He then turned to a study of the law, graduating the University of Michigan Law School in May of 1876. That same year he formed a law partnership

with Samuel W. Hopkins, until 1878 when Hopkins was elected State Representative and Devereaux was elected Isabella County Prosecuting Attorney. In 1882, he formed Hance and Devereaux law firm with J. W. Hance, specializing in general real estate and loaning business. Together and separately, both Devereaux and Hance became prominent landowners and developers in Mt. Pleasant, making some additions to the town, *see Appendix 1, page 235.* In 1895, Devereaux built a brick building that still bears his name in the 100 block of East Broadway to house his firm's offices, replacing a building built in 1883 and burned in March 1895.

The house at 514 South Main became the home of Dr. Albert T. and Ella Getchell, *see 304 South Main*, following Devereaux's 1911 death. Dr. Getchell was then in his mid-60s and the front room of this house allowed him smaller space to continue his limited practice until his death.

From 1930 until 1945, the house became the home of CMU's Dr. Eugene C. Rowe, *right*, who came to Mt. Pleasant in 1902, as Central's first PhD holder, to head Central Michigan Normal School's Psychology Department, retiring in 1936. Rowe was the United States Army Chief Psychological Examiner in World War I, helping develop the Army's Alpha Test, predecessor to the Intelligence Quotient (IQ) Test. Before his 1946 death, he helped pioneer the eugenics movement. Rowe Hall on the Central's campus was dedicated in his name in 1955.

Rowe's family sold the house to the Ambler family, who sold it to David and Mark Coyne, who remodeled it and earned the 1985 Mt. Pleasant City Improvement Award. The house was also selected as a Centennial Home when Mt. Pleasant celebrated the 100th Anniversary of its charter as a city in 1989. In 2012, the address, *left,* is home to the Phi Sigma Sigma Sorority.

515 South Main Built in 1870 by Edward Coburn, the house was sold in 1875 to attorney, later judge, Peter F. Dodds, *right,* and his wife Minnie. Here they raised their son Fai B. Dodds.

In 1918, the house was sold to Albert Bissell's widow Electra M., who lived there until her 1927 death.

Mt. Pleasant Postmaster Rae Hooker, bought the house in 1929 sold it in 1940 to M & M Bar, 112 West Michigan, owners Medard and Martha Claus, who lived at 214 ½ West Michigan before moving to *503 North Arnold.* The home was rented by oil worker F. R. Sahrot in the 1950s and to Gase Bakery salesman Robert Gase and his wife teacher Dorelyn who lived there along with children Debra and Robert in the 1960s.

The Claus' son, Ace Hardware owner Michael Claus and his teacher wife Jean took possession of the house and remodeled it in 1968. Here they raised daughters Jennifer and Anna.

Michael and Jean Claus sold the home to Vern and Rosemary Hoag in 2009.

601 South Main, shown above in 1906, was built in 1904 by lumber/banking magnate John S. Weidman, *below*, this was his residence until his 1919 death, and family resided there until 1943. John S. Weidman was born in Kenockee Township of St. Clair County, Michigan in 1852, one of twelve children. The family resided there until 1866, when they moved to Mecosta County just south of Big Rapids. He began his working life as a river log driver at age 16 and until age 26 worked as a log runner during the summer and a timber camp foreman during the winters. By careful saving, in 1876 he was able to purchase ten-acre tract in Hinton Township of Mecosta County, gradually expanding it to a 600-acre farm. In 1877, he bought and timbered a tract of "homestead land" in Mecosta County, rising rapidly in the lumber business world, to begin operations in Michigan and Wisconsin.

He married Margaret A. Mitchell at Big Rapids and they raised six children: Lenora D., Mildred A., John S. Jr., Robert, Lucille, and Evan.

In 1892, John Weidman bought a tract of 8,000 acres in Isabella County and built saw, shingle and planing mills, founding the village of Weidman and cut an average of ten million board feet of lumber a year for many years.

In 1903, Weidman bought a private bank in Mt. Pleasant and incorporated the Isabella County State Bank, and in 1904 built his Mt. Pleasant home, which in 1943 Miss Mildred Weidman, a director of the Isabella County State Bank, sold the house to Sohio Petroleum Company. Sohio maintained offices on the top floor while renting apartments on the floors below.

According to city directories, later residents of the house included pilot Paul G. Finetti, his wife Louise, as well as, from the early 1950s until mid-1960s. Capper Publications Sales Superintendent Lou Jensen, his wife Rosetta and children Diane and Lou Jr. Jensen later moved to *628 South Arnold Street* in Mt. Pleasant

In 2012, *below,* the address is home to Zeta Tau Alpha Fraternity, with ownership residing with Gamma Micron of Zeta Tau Alpha HC listed at *205 North Kinney*, Mt. Pleasant Michigan, according to the Assessing Service software on the City of Mt. Pleasant website.

604 South Main, above, was probably built during the 1879 to 1903 ownership- by William N. and Minnie Brown, who assigned it in 1903 to the Baptist Convention, who owned the property until 1923. In 1923, longtime Mt. Pleasant Attorney, Virgil William McClintic, whose offices were a block away at 500 South Main, and his wife Leah purchased this home. Virgil McClintic died in 1972. For a while during the 1970s, the address was home to Central Michigan University professor Ulysses D. Knott, Jr. and his wife Barbara D, along with sons Ulysses III and Robert. In late 1970s, it was home to attorney William M. McClintic. In 1984, the house sold to Eugene and Virginia Balogh, who sold in 1988 to Zeta Rho Housing Corporation.

619 South Main, right, was built in 1890 by Joshua and Frances Ivinson, who sold in 1891 to Joseph Deuel. From 1926 until 1942, the house belonged to meat cutter Frank M. Keenan and his wife Helen. In 1942, Harry E. Tope, whose family, through Earl Harry Tope Jr., owned it until 1971 when it sold to teacher Ronald Johnson and his teacher wife Karen. In 2002, Pat McGuirk, Jr. assigned the house to the Nancy Jo McGuirk Living Trust, which in turn assigned it to Quality Apartments LLC in 2005.

702 South Main This modified Italianate style home with a pyramidal roof, north side bay window facing Cherry Street and ornate bracket trim on the gently arched wraparound porch facing Main Street is punctuated by a yard trimmed with painted fieldstone. The house was built in 1890 by attorney Daniel E. Lyon, a real estate, insurance specialist who, with partner Samuel W. Hopkins in the loan business made $100,000 in loans in 1893. The astounding sum of loans so impressed Isaac A Fancher that he mentioned it in his book *Isabella County: Past and Present.*

The Lyon family retained ownership of the home until 1924 when it was sold to William F. Prior and his wife Chresa, who raised daughter Mary there. Mary, who was later Mary Dawson lived here, as did carpenter Ernest E, Prior and his wife Virgelene.

In 1967, the Prior family sold to Donald B. and Joyce K. Brown, who sold in 1969 to Gary and Roger Faculck, who sold in 1977 to James Barwick, a large property owner and landlord.

James Barwick sold to the Robert J. Neyer Trust, who sold to the Higgemboom family. In 1997, the longtime rental property became that of M & D Investments, who sold to Jeff Jakeway another large landowner and landlord, who sold in 2009 to Ames LLC.

Renters along the way have been; Vance and Emily Orr in the late 1930s; CMU student Richard Murray and his Mt. Pleasant High School physical education instructor wife Arlene J. in the 1960s; and Bradley Chartier in the late 1970s.

814 South Main was built in 1914 by Central Michigan Normal Professor John Kelley and his wife Minta E. John Kelley joined the faculty of Central in 1898 and in the course of his career would be Superintendent of Normal's training school *(where future teachers would teach local and faculty members family children under supervision to train for real world teaching)* Registrar and Rural Education Department head. Here the Kelleys raised two sons, Spencer and Paul, and a daughter, Elizabeth. Kelley died of a sudden heart attack at Christmastime, 1925, and Minta lived in the house until her 1936 death.

Mt. Pleasant attorney Gerald J. Cotter, *below in 1943*, and his wife Altha bought the house in 1936. After receiving his law degree from University of Detroit, Gerald Cotter practiced law in Mt. Pleasant for 50 years and in the course of his career served as Isabella County Prosecuting Attorney, Chairman of the Michigan State Board of Appeals, and Michigan Senator. He also was the first person in Mt. Pleasant to own a Rolls Royce automobile, a distinction not matched until modern times by apartment landlord Jim McGuirk. Here the Cotters raised Gerald J. Jr., Thomas, Joyce, Ruth, Mary Ellen, Carol Ann and Lisa.

The Cotters sold the house in 1952 to Delta Sigma Phi and then the property underwent a series of ownerships by: James Barwick; William and Marcia Kennedy; and Gregory and Dorothy Bunting to become the property of Epsilon Gamma Chapter in 1987.

916 South Main has been an academic address since it was built in 1906 by Ira A. Beddow, *below*, on property he had acquired from Dr. Eugene C. Rowe, *see 614 South Main, pages 155-156*, who bought the lot from Mr. Charles T. Grawn, *see 301 East High*, *page 96*, both of whom did not build there but bought existing homes elsewhere. Beddow, Grawn and Rowe would later have buildings named for them that still exist on the Mt. Pleasant campus of Central Michigan University. Ira Beddow came to Central in 1906 after teaching in Detroit, Bay City and at Olivet College. He began teaching history during Central's summer session and joined the faculty in the fall as a speech instructor. He headed the Department of Speech and Reading from 1906 to 1939.

Ira Beddow and his wife Theresa would have two daughters and four sons here. Theresa Beddow died suddenly of a heart attack at 58 years old in November of 1928 and Beddow lived on in the house until retirement, and then moved to St. Petersburg, Florida, where he died in 1950. He sold the house to oilman Evart G. Thompson and his wife Angeline in a sale finalized in 1948.

The Thompsons sold to Central Michigan University's Alpha Chi Omega fraternity in 1969.

1028 South Main in 1893 The opening of Central Michigan Normal School and Business Institute in 1892 brought about a huge surge of additions to the City of Mt. Pleasant, mostly southward of High Street. "Six additions to the city have been platted in the year 1892" read the November 25, 1892, *Enterprise*. " These six additions aggregate 474 lots distributed as follows: Brown's Addition 68 lots, Martin's Addition 22 lots, College Hill Addition 38 lots, Normal School Addition 228 lots, Bennett & Burrows Addition 68 lots, and Hance's Addition 50 lots. The erection of houses has begun on all but two, while the proportion of lots remaining in the hands of the owners platting the same is much less than half.". In June of 1893, the 96 lot Hopkins & Partridge's Addition between Mission and Kinney streets south of High was added to the city, with Arnold Street extended south through the center of the Addition. Stimulated by the new Normal School, Mt. Pleasant was on the grow.

Housing for Central students was an issue, there being none on campus, and Central Principal Charles F. R. Bellows was continually appealing to townsfolk to house members of the growing student body.

Apparently not content with the result, Bellows with Thomas Tonkin, Tobias Bergy, along with John and George Butcher formed a partnership to build and operate a boarding house in the Normal School Addition on Main Street. Announcement in the February 21, 1893, *Enterprise* said "The building will be 32 by 60 feet, two stories and will give room for caring for twenty to thirty students. It will be heated by steam and lighted by electricity and will cost from $1,500 to $2000."

Newspapers touted the progress of the Normal Boarding House, *above just after opening*, throughout the year and on Wednesday, December 20, 1893, a housewarming party was held at the building. "oysters will be served and a musical program will be given. The managers will furnish free transportation for all parts of the city to those buying tickets. This will be a fine opportunity to inspect the building and contribute a mite to make other improvements" the December 18, 1893, *Enterprise* reported breathlessly.

In those days before "investigative reporting, no one seemed to question the propriety of the head of the Normal School investing in a boarding house for his charges. "There was no hint of conflict of interest" John Cumming says in his *The First Hundred Years – Central Michigan University 1892-1992*. It is curious to note, however, that when Central Michigan Normal School became a state college, Charles McKenny was hired as its principal.

In 1896, with the aforementioned partnership apparently dissolved, builder John Ryan sold the boarding house to John and Mary Zank. The boarding house passed through several owner's hands until acquisition in 1938 by Peter S. Mogg, his wife Gracie, and Harold Taylor and his wife Bernadine. Both Mogg and Taylor are listed as mechanics in the 1939-1940 Mt. Pleasant City Directory. By the 1947-48 Mt. Pleasant City Directory, only the Moggs are listed as owners and Peter is listed as managers of the Pete Mogg Leonard service and gasoline station at 301 East Broadway. Peter Mogg died in 1969 and Gracie in 1969.

The early 1970s carry no record of occupancy for the house but student names began to appear as residents from the mid-1970s until 1985 when the Michigan Christian Ministries bought it from J & J Apartments.

In 2012, after 119 years of service to the students of Central, the house remains as His House Christian Fellowship, a non-denominational Christian ministry committed to the campus and community of Central Michigan University for Christ and establishing a thriving New Testament Church, according to their online information.

202 to 222 South Mission By the time this late 1950s photograph was taken with Geroux Motors, the corner to 220 South Mission, would later be the home of the Tastee Freeze soft ice cream store, *far right above*, took up the space once occupied by houses at **202 to 216 South Mission**.

Occupants of these addresses through the years included:

202 South Mission – Mrs. Dora Vining, Mary Ruth Crippin, Walter L. Moyer, Robert Greynolds, Alfonso Fortino and the Tastee Freeze.

210 South Mission – Minor Demoond, James and Margaret Corcoran, Archey and White Auto Sales, Isabella County Credit Union, Biggby Coffee.

216 South Mission – Lorenzo and Sarah Warner, Sarah Campbell, Geroux Motors and Dairy Queen.

222 South Mission – From 1925 until 1985, this house was under the ownership of the Lawrence S. and Ione Tanner and their son, Maynard. Lawrence Tanner was born in Mt. Pleasant in 1894. He owned a Shell gasoline filling station at 1018 West Broadway for forty years and was a member of the Mt. Pleasant Fire Department for thirty years, serving as Fire Chief from 1952 until 1959 retirement. Lawrence died in 1975, Maynard in 1993 and Ione in 1994.

In 1985, the property was sold to William and Nancy Boutell and in 1990 it was sold to TBD Limited.

1100-1200 Block of South Mission Street (then Road) in 1958 This look from the air at a portion of South Mission in the late 1950s is part of a photograph of Rowe Hall on the Central Michigan campus at its opening.

For landmark sake **1106 South Mission,** the large rectangular building just off-center in the scene is the Michigan State Highway Department, now headquarters office of Michigan Special Olympics.

Immediately across the 2-lane Mission, left to right up the diagonal road in the photo are: **1119 South Mission**, home of Brazos Oil and Gas Company draftsman Hilton C. E. Ux and his wife Katherine along with sons Howard and Allen; then **1141 South Mission** the home of Howard Wilton, and his Bob's Barber Shop, his wife Leona , along with sons Howard and Allen; then **1143 South Mission** the home of Turner Petroleum roustabout Fred Scholl, his wife Zelda, as well as sons Charles, Steven and Gary.

1203 South Mission, Marsh Monument Company along with the home of Dorothy West, and Michigan Consolidated Gas finish the east side of this view at **1205 South Mission.** The Michigan Consolidated Gas office building now houses Family Footcare of Mid-Michigan, among others.

On the west side of Mission Street, right of the Highway Department building, are: **1206 South Mission**, home of Art Periard, owner of Chippewa Lanes Recreation, *at 111 ½ South Main Street, eventually to locate at this location*, his wife Doris, along with children Pamela, Arthur and Ronald**; 1216 South Mission**, home of Gulf Oil Superintendent Howard Wright and his wife Dorothy; **1220 South Mission**, home of retired judge Walter S. Horn and his wife Bernice; and **1224 South Mission**, home of State Highway Department mechanic Kenneth E. Dargitz, his wife Helen and daughters Darlene and Diane.

108 South Oak was built in 1910 by Samuel L. Harris, second generation of the Harris brothers, William E, and John A., who built Harris Milling Company around the corner at 411 East Broadway in 1872. The mill ground grist and flour, then made pancake and prepared biscuit mixes, as well as dog, dairy, trout and turkey feed. A cement dam installed on the Chippewa River by the Harris family created a millrun to power the plant with electricity. When the water was high, the excess electricity was sold to the City of Mt. Pleasant, from which the mill bought electricity when water levels were low.

The mill closed more than 100 years after opening and was abandoned. Its tower stood through a 1990 fire. The mill's tower was toppled and the site cleared in 1999.

The Harris family owned this house until 1947, when it was sold to car dealer Norman LaBelle, later to found the Pixie Drive-In restaurant, and his wife Loraine. Other owner/occupants included career Michigan Department of Conservation Geological Survey Division geologist Garland Ells and his wife Freda; Howard Tractor Sales mechanic Evert Sheldon and his wife Donna; and Larry Hill.

In 2003, Ethel Swain sold the house to Mt. Pleasant businessman Norman Curtiss and his wife Joanne, owners of Curtiss Pro Hardware at 118 South Main and the Downtown Dollar Store at 103 East Broadway, among others.

312-318 South Oak Oak Tree Apartments were built on the three acres once occupied by the St. Charles Roman Catholic Church, the first Roman Catholic Church in Mt. Pleasant, a wood frame building built in 1875. St. Charles was officiated by Father John McCarthy, who died in 1885. The new pastor, Father James Crowley, saw that the parish was growing more rapidly than the church could accommodate and purchased the entire 300 block of East Michigan Street for $1,500 in 1887. The old wood church was moved there and building of a new church began. Oak Tree Apartments were erected in 1973.

319 South Oak was built by John M. Tinney in 1891. It was rented by Harris Milling Company's John W. and Rosetta Showalter in the 1940s. John W. was later Service Manager for J. F. Battle's automobile dealership at 706 east Broadway and still later filled the same position for Krapohl Ford at 114 Court Street. John W. died in 1974 and Rosetta in 1980, whereupon the house went to rentals.

401 South Oak is one of the more modern design homes that dot the east side of the 300 and 400 blocks of Oak Street. The house was built by Roosevelt Refinery President C. L. McGuire in 1938. The McGuire family owned the house until 1945, during which one renter was E. Allan Morrow, a leaseman for Roosevelt, and his wife Bernice. From 1945-1959, the house belonged to Leonard Pipeline leaseman John Devine. Midway Supply Company's Don Mitchell and his wife Gladys lived there in 1964. Later owners included: Dow Chemical Laboratory Superintendent Laurence Lyon and his wife Marlene; Bonnell Furniture Carpet Manager David E. Barnes and his wife Barbara (Westbrook); and, since 1992, Gregory J. Fogle.

715 South Oak Built in 1903 by Samuel D. Brown, this recently re-sided house was the 1938-1962 home of cook Anna B. Snyder, then Church of Christ Pastor John Butts, later John Hoddy, then Richard Nethers.

514 South Oak was built in 1904 by Charles L. Woodruff and for many years was a two apartment rental with residents including: laborer H. K. Abernathy and his wife Margurita with truck driver Hugh Peterson and his wife Leona downstairs in 1940; From 1942 on, the Cotton family have owned the house, beginning with electrician Rudy J. Cotton as owner, who owned Cotton Electric company at 117 South Main Street and would ultimately become City of Mt. Pleasant electrical inspector rental, His wife Frauleen, a cafeteria assistant at Mt. Pleasant High School. Rudy and Frauleen raised son Robert and daughter Betty , *below* in front of the house in 1943, and following Rudy's 1966 death, Frauleen continued to live there with Bob Cotton and his wife Kathleen, and sons Randy and Rickey. Frauleen Cotton died in 1987.

Three generations of the William Cowden family pose in front of 614 Oak Street in pre-1908 photograph from Hattie Cowden-Froggett-Hart's granddaughter, Pat Wilmot of Shepherd. Right to left are: Front Row – Marion and Marie Froggett, granddaughters of William Cowden, seated; Back Row - Hattie Froggett, daughter, with Susan Cowden.

614 South Oak was built in 1897 by Clifton and Julia D. Dean. William Cowden bought the house in 1901 and it remained in the family, through assignments to Hattie Cowden-Froggett-Hart, who moved into the house after the 1946 death of her husband automobile dealer and bus and taxi service owner Clarence E. Hart in 1940. Hattie lived there until 1968, when the house was sold to Albert F. and Landis Haas and continued as a rental property. Through the years, the address was also home to Charles Baker – 1939; Harold J. Wilmot and his wife Patricia – 1958; and Vance E. Hoffmeyer with his wife Madeline J.

Ultimately, as with many older homes in the south end of Mt. Pleasant, the structure was replaced by an apartment building, *right*, in 1983.

315 South Pine This classic gable front and wing family home in the National Folk Home style with a wraparound porch as built in 1887 by Michael and Lizzie Donahue, who sold in 1902 to John J. Cowen.

Jacob and Nancy Rowe bought the house form Cowen in 1919 and in 1924 sold it to Ann Arbor Railroad Depot Freight Officer Lester Elder and his wife Blanche A. Here the Elders raised daughters Dorothy and Betty.

Shoe repairman and cleaner Sam Lirones bought the house as a rental income property in 1950. Through the years, Lirones rented the house to: newcomers from New England Central Michigan College Mathematic Professor Harold Zeoli and wife Dorothy in the 1950s; Pelletier Electric electrician William H. Leasher and his wife Mary K. in the 1960s; and CMU artist-designer Eugene Church and his wife Barbara, then Mary Wise in the 1970s. Sam Lirones died in 1979 but the family retained ownership until 1988 when purchase was finalized by Gary and Candice Conant.

When the photo above was taken for this book, the Conants were in the middle of a repaint job, thus the ladder in front. However, we couldn't resist taking a picture of the two fanciful planters on the front porch, left.

401 South Pine Street Built in 1879 by Salania Bellinger, the house sold in 1892 to Lewis and Hattie Wardwell, who sold in 1902 to John T. Landon, *below*.

The inset to this photo of Jesse Landon and his wife in front of the family home, *above,* shows Jesse's father John T. Landon tending his garden at the ornate residence. John T. came to Chippewa Township, Isabella County at age 22 from his native Canada in September, 1862. He worked a year for $15 a month and board for he and his wife. In 1863, he went into debt to buy 40 acres and in 1873, now a prominent landowner, lumberman and farmer, he built the county's first brick structure as a Chippewa Township residence. An avid hunter, John T. Landon's hunting exploits were reported area wide breathlessly by newspapers in his later life. He was living in the Pine Street house when he died in 1912, one of 6 properties he owned in Mt. Pleasant.

Later owners included Joseph Schwartz, who sold to Michael and Serenity Brady in 1997, who sold to David and Deniege London in 2004, who in turn sold to Robert and Denise Fanning in 2008.

The house was restored in the 1990s and in 2012 retains the charm of the original home

410 South Pine This Folk National style side gable home with a center dormer and porch was built in 1893 by John Sweet, the house was sold in 1909 to retired farmer Thomas Carroll. Following Thomas Carroll's 1916 death, his son Patrick and his wife Hannah Carroll became owners of the property until 1937 when it was assigned to their son Lloyd C. Carroll and his wife Dorothy, who lived there until the mid 1940s, *see 815 West Broadway*, page 228.

The Carrolls sold to Main Street Barber Shop, 201 North Main Street, owner Leroy Neier and his wife Mary. Leroy, the name sake of Neier Road on the west side of Mt. Pleasant, died in 1970 in a home on Neier Road. Mary, in her later years worked at American Cleaners in alterations. Here Leroy and Mary raised Richard and Lois.

In 1983, the home sold to John Robertson and Nina Monahan, who sold to David Russell Fisher in 1992, who sold in 1999 to Clara Agrady.

201-203 South University, left to right These two properties passed through a number of hands on a street that was variously called Church Street, then Normal Avenue, *later College and now University*, before this 1919 photograph was taken as a site picture preparatory to construction on the site. Note the puddled state of the avenue.

In 1870, Jared Doughty of the Doughty family of early Mt. Pleasant merchants, bought the properties from Abigail Babbitt Whitney. He lived at 201 and rented out 203, where a family named Anderson lived in the 1910s. In the fall of 1869, Jared and Wilkinson Doughty, brothers from Van Buren County, arrived in Mount Pleasant. Here they found no tinsmith or hardware merchant so they decided to set up shop. Jared was a skillful tinsmith and had been in business before. They opened a store in space rented from Isaac A Fancher at the northeast corner of Broadway and Main Streets. The Doughty brothers prospered and became, for the rest of the century and well into the next, two of Mount Pleasants leading merchants. In 1875, after a devastating downtown fire obliterated the wooden structures lining the north side of Broadway, the Doughtys built a brick structure across the street to the south.

In 1916, Jared Doughty sold the properties to the United States government for construction of a new post office. World War I delayed erection of the building, *below in the 1940*s, until 1919. The building was offices for the Mt. Pleasant School System from the 1960s until the 1980s and has been private office space since.

206 South University is located on a lot that was once a part of the location of Mt. Pleasants first school. Jennie King bought the property from Union Township School District 1 in 1883 and assessment records indicate that the house was built in 1894.

For 110 years, a Johnson has lived here. In 1902, the house was bought by Mt. Pleasant shoe merchant John H. Johnson and his wife Mary C. Johnson. Originally from Petersboro, Canada, Johnson came to Mt. Pleasant during the town's lumber era and ultimately entered in partnership with his brother James to form Johnson Shoe Company at 114 East Broadway. He married Mary Epple in 1897. Here they raised Lucille, Helen, Beatrice, James, and Philip R. John H. Johnson died in 1930 and was so respected in the community that all downtown businesses closed during his funeral. Helen lived in the house until her 1954 death, having sold in 1951 to her son Philip R. and his wife Dorothy.

Dr. Philip R. Johnson had graduated from what is now Central Michigan University in 1927 with a Bachelors degree, then University of Michigan Medical School in 1931, completing his residency at Harper Hospital in Detroit in 1932. From the Michigan State Medical Society, he received an associate fellowship in post graduate education in 1938 and a fellowship in 1942. He was a family doctor, with offices at this location for many of his medically practicing years, in the area from 1932 until 1979, along with serving as university physician for 10 years and a physician for the Mt. Pleasant Regional Center for Developmental Disabilities.

Here the Johnsons raised Philip, John, Robert, Anne, Janet M., Helen K., Mary and Margaret. Dr. Philip Johnson died in 1985.

302 South University The base cobblestone structure law office complex was built in 1901 by a lady believed to be Mt. Pleasants first female medical doctor, Dr. Amy Holcomb, who had the building designed to accommodate her medical practice. The 1948 Mt. Pleasant City Directory shows the property owned by O. Holcomb, likely a descendant. By 1963, the Michigan Department of Corrections shared the building with owner Realtor George J. Marks. In 1981, Andrew Marks sold the building to attorney Tim Taylor, who converted an upstairs apartment to his office. In 1987, *above,* Taylor added a 3,500 square foot wing to the building, then co-owned with attorney Tom Hall, Jr., and then the building was home to the legal practices of Taylor, Daniel Pyscher, Daniel O'Neil, Tom Hall, John Lewis, Paul Chamberlain, William T. Ervin and Joseph Barberi.

In 2012, right, the Cornerstone Professional Center home to the offices of attorneys Becky Bolles, Tom Hall Jr., Jeffrey Lynch, Daniel O'Neil and Daniel H. Pyscher.

330 South University In 1909, G. Jay Stinson came to Mt. Pleasant and opened a funeral home on Broadway Street, later moving into a building on South Normal Street.

Stinson operated the funeral home there for several years with his sons under the name Stinson and Sons Funeral Home, before building a new funeral home in 1940 at 330 South Normal Street, which was renamed College Street, and eventually University Avenue. The building was dedicated in early 1941, and has been in continuous use as a funeral home since then. In addition to operating the funeral home, an ambulance service was also operated from this same building. Stinson Funeral Home was the last funeral home in the county to have an ambulance service, when it was discontinued in 1963.

Stinson passed away in 1952, and his son, Russell continued to operate the funeral home until his retirement in 1973, when long time employee Harry Helms and his wife Alice purchased the funeral home and named it Stinson-Helms.

Helms started working at the funeral home in the early 1940's part time while attending Central Michigan College. He served his country during World War II, and came back to Mt. Pleasant and returned to work at the Stinson Funeral Home. After attending mortuary school at Wayne State University, he returned to work at the funeral home. He passed away in 1980, and his wife, Alice continued operation of the Helms Funeral Home until her retirement in 2010, when she sold the funeral home to long time employee, Sherman Rowley and his wife Shirley. Sherm has been with the funeral home since November 1979. The name was changed to Rowley Funeral Home in August, 2010.

319 South University Around 1890 a group of Mt. Pleasant citizens became interested in the Christian Science Church movement. They organized loosely, and formally chartered on January 15, 1891, as the Mt. Pleasant Christian Science Church, meeting in various private homes. They found that they needed a church building and finally selected and purchased the home and site of the Richard Balmer home on Lot 8 of Block 33 (319 South Church Street) on the 18th day of July, 1907.

The residence was remodeled into a very convenient and spacious church, very prettily finished, and decorated with beautiful windows. On April 19, 1908, the church was dedicated.

In 1981, several art groups in Mt. Pleasant merged to create Art Reach of Mid Michigan and acquired the Christian Science Church building, which was transformed into an art center.

In 2000, Art Reach purchased a building at 111 East Broadway, which became the organization's office and gift shop.

In 2010, the building next door at 113 East Broadway became available and was purchased by Art Reach of Mid Michigan and converted to a gallery and meeting room, with offices in the back. Art Reach moved all operations to Art Reach on Broadway in July, 2010, with a grand opening held in mid-August, 2010.

The 319 South University location became the home of the Unitarian Universalist Fellowship of Central Michigan Church in July, 2010.

404 South University Normal Avenue had just become College Street when jeweler Edward A. Voisin of Voisin Jewelers at 112 East Broadway, and his wife Clara built this home in 1928, *shown above shortly after construction.* Here they raised sons Joseph F., Walter E. and Leo E. , as well as daughters Kathryn, Lillian E., Ruth M., Dorothy M., and Rita A. Edward Voisin died in 1956.

In 1958, Clara Voisin turned the house over to the Presbyterian Church and in 1963 it was purchased by Dow Chemical Supervisor Clair S. Bingham and his wife Dorothy, a nurse at Central Michigan Community Hospital. In 1998, the home sold to Alma College Associate Professor Clyde Gehrig and his wife Janet.

Later owners of the house, *shown below in 2012*, have included Maggie Badovinac, James and Ida Monroe, as well as Geoffrey and Mariana Quick. Note the windows of the foyer at the right and above the front door have been "squared" by remodeling.

412 South University The property originally belonged to George Day and was part of the Bentley Addition to Mt. Pleasant. The house was built on Lot 3 of Block 4 in 1904 by James and Nellie McEntee on Normal Street, which became College Street, then University Avenue in 1968. Other owner/occupants included David and Magaret Crowley in 1920; Danies and Lizzie Dibble in 1922; Charles W. and Lettie R. Prout in 1930, and Charles and Amelia Myers in 1934.

In 1941, Michigan oil and gas drilling contractor Leon G. Thompson, *right*, and his wife Edith bought the house.

After Leon's 1950s death, Edith continued to live there until 1994, when she sold to Kristin M. Moutsatson, now owner of the Book Shelf bookstore at 1014 South Mission.

417 South University Note the mock-keystone upper story Italianate hooded windows of this house built in 1894 by George and Henrietta Day, managers of the Bennett House Hotel. In 1897, the Days built a new, larger home at 404 *North Main, see page 53,* and sold this property to James Armstrong.

In 1932, Augustine W. Lynch and his wife Agnes bought the property and it remained in family ownership until 1977. A. W. "Gus" Lynch came to Michigan with his parents, Mr. and Mrs. William Lynch, who settled in Rosebush. A Central Michigan graduate, Lynch was teacher-superintendent at Mackinac Island school for many years, and was later employed by Benzinger Brothers Publishers, then managed the Catholic School Publication Department of Scott, Foreman company at Chicago. The Lynch's had one daughter, Margaret, and three sons: Thomas, Richard, and John. Agnes Lynch died in 1953 and "Gus" Lynch died in 1986, having moved from this address to *304 East Wisconsin.*

Lynch sold this house in 1977 to Mt. Pleasant attorney William M. McClintic and his wife Pauline S.

In 1986, the house was sold to Nancy Lou Stronge and Connie Lee Navarre, in 1990 to Christopher and Catherine Wojtowkz, in 1976 to James F. Haupt and his wife Kathleen, and in 2000 to Dale Betts.

Along the way, renter occupants to the house have included: Go-Marathon service station Manager Howard F. Frick; Flemings Apparel for Men shop, 117 E. Broadway, owner Arthur H. Fleming and his wife Mae; and Donald W. and Kay F. Dusenbury.

Scott A. and Sue Ellen Deni-Owen bought the house in 2002.

502 South University was built in 1875 by William H. Richmond and his wife Maria. William Richmond served as a lieutenant in the Civil War. He and his brother John were two out of 232 men who returned to their St. Lawrence County, New York, home from 1,100 men in his division. The Richmonds came to the settlement of Mt. Pleasant in 1875 and that same year he was elected one of the trustees when the settlement was organized as a village. Here in this house, William and Maria raised sons John and Berne, of Ann Arbor, Michigan, and Terra Haute, Indiana, at the time of William's 1908 death.

In 1909, the house was acquired by lumberman, farmer and livestock dealer turned real estate man Charles J. Myers and his wife Amelia. Here they raise two sons, Walter and Stacy and daughter Mrs. Myron Elmore *(first name not reported)*. Amelia Myers died in 1937. Charles sold the house to Mrs. Laura I. Cramer, who died there in the mid-1940s, when her daughter Julia C. Shirley became owner of the house. Julia Shirley, Society Editor (*right from a 1943 cartoon round-up of the Isabella County Times-News staff*) raised son William there who is now a local attorney. In 1971, she sold the house to Beta XI of PI Kappa Phi, a CMU fraternity.

In 1978, the house belonged to James E. and Donna Born, who sold it to William and Sally Antaya. The house went on to be used as an apartment house. Later the house was sold in early 2012 to Allison Quast and Michael Lents, Jr., who at this writing are returning it to a single family dwelling.

505 South University was built in 1890, according to the City of Mt. Pleasant Assessing Service online software, probably on speculation by either David G. Robinson or I. A. Fancher. Either way, in 1891 the house was sold by Fancher to Elizabeth Brown Hursh.

Elizabeth married John M. Hush in 1837 in up-state New York and in 1855; she came with him from Clyde, New York, to the wilderness area that would become Isabella County. They settled on their 80 acres in a log cabin believed to have been located near where present day Warriner Hall stands on the Mt. Pleasant campus of Central Michigan University. The population of the area grew rapidly and the Hursh family grew with it. They had 11 children. Elizabeth and John are pictured, *left*.

John invested in a number of properties. Property records show more than 100 Isabella County land transactions in his name. He bought the Morton House, Mt. Pleasant's first hotel at the northwest corner of today's Main and Broadway streets in 1864, and then sold it to build the Hursh House hotel in the booming northeastern Isabella County lumber town of Loomis. Elizabeth went to Loomis to run the hotel. In 1877, John died, leaving Elizabeth with three young children at home and the hotel she continued to run with the help of the older children. In 1890, she returned to Mt. Pleasant to live in this house until her 1892 death at 73 years old. The house stayed in the family until 1901 when it was sold to a Thomas Barber; in 1916 to Blanche Brown; and to a successive stream of fourteen more owners since, primarily used as a rental property, which it remains to modern times.

508 and 510 South University are both built of "Mt. Pleasant brick", a pale yellow local manufactured style seen in many late 19th Century constructed homes.

508 South University, left The property was built in 1885 commonly owned with *502 South University* next door to the north until 1949, and was probably built by William H. Richmond as a duplex rental property, note an outside stairway to an upstairs apartment. A popular rental to oil people. Driller George D. Westbrook and his wife Lilly L. rented the downstairs and lived there from the mid 1930s until his 1956 death at this house, and her early 1960s death here. In 1939, gas engineers Ollie Gaterell was also a rental resident. In 1964, the home became a fraternity house for Beta X1 of PI Kappa PI and was later converted to student housing. Greydon and Linda Hyde owned the home in the early 1990s and sold it to John Faust in 1996.

510 South University, below, was built in 1889 by Samuel R. Morrison, who sold in 1890 to Oscar F. Sheldon and his wife Sarah. The Sheldons owned the home until 1926, when it was sold to Daniel Kane. In the 1930s, Donald Baize of Roosevelt Oil owned the house and in 1945 drayman, construction worker and then Isabella County Deputy Sheriff Ernest Peters and his wife Mildred M. bought the house. The Peters would raise daughter Barbara J., as well as sons Thomas E. and Kenneth L. there. Ernest died in 1963 and Mildred followed in 2004. In 2005, the Peters estate sold the house to William E. O'Dell and O'Dell Investments.

509 South University, left, was built in 1894 by Peter and Rebecca Gardner. In 1939, it was owned by Beulah Fletcher and later it became became the home of her son, independent oil operator Russell Fletcher and his wife, an attendant at the Mt. Pleasant State Home and Training School. Here they raised Lucinda, Katherine, Kane and Thomas. In 1965, the house sold to Mt. Pleasant Public Library librarian Lloyd R. Hansen and his Isabella County Friend of the Court wife Beth. From 1972 until 1983, Pastor Robert F. Garrels called the house home, until it was sold to John Anger and Gayl Stamris. Since 1987, ownership has resided with Peter and Marie Koper.

512 South University, right Built in 1890 by Oscar F. Sheldon and his wife Sarah, the house remained home to them until 1902. In 1922, the house was sold to Mt. Pleasant City office's Albert Carroll and his teacher wife Bertha. Here they would raise Barbara, William, Robert, Mary Jo and Shirley.

In 1957, the Carrolls sold the house to Ferro Stamping Company Foreman Albert L. Neff, later a United States Postal Service employee and his wife Madeline, an employee of Central Michigan University. Here the Neffs would raise Patrick, Catherine, Barbara, Bernard and Michael. As the Neff children grew and left home, the Neff created a rental apartment upstairs. Alfred Leo Neff died in 1991.

604 South University was built in 1884 by building contractor John Hidey, who lived next door at *610 South University*, and sold to Mary Richmond. In 1911, the house sale was completed to Owen and Jenny Keith. Who sold in 1920 to Jessie and Eliza Brasengton, and in 1925 the property was sold to Elizabeth Dillon.

College Services Garage Manager for Central Michigan College Harold W. Hislop and his wife Lucille bought the house in 1938.

Former Assistant District Manager for National Cylinder Gas Company of Ferndale, Michigan, William G. Kelly and his wife Marianne moved to Mt. Pleasant, bought the house and built Kelly Welding Supply at 107 Leaton Street in 1956. While in the Detroit area they had raised sons Jerry and James, along with daughters Maureen and Catherine. William G. Kelly also operated the Mt. Pleasant branch of the Michigan Secretary of State office from 1970-1975 and was Chairman of the Isabella County Democratic Party. Active in the Knights of Columbus both Mt. Pleasant and Ferndale, Kelly was Grand Master of the Michigan State Knights of Columbus 1959-1960. The 1977 Fourth Degree Knights of Columbus class statewide was named for him in 1977.

Later, the Kellys would sell the house to Gamma Omicron of Zeta and move into the Kelly Welding Supply building until "Bill" Kelly's 1982 death.

Gamma Omicron. of Zeta sold to Patrick H. and Nancy Jo McGuirk in 2002 and it was assigned to Quality Apartments in 2005.

610 South University, shown above in 1906, with its distinctive ornate latticework trim on the front porch, was built by builder John T. Hidey, *right*, in 1884 upon his arrival in Mt. Pleasant. The feature became a hallmark of residences built by Hidey. As a builder, Hidey was to make his mark on Mt. Pleasant as the builder of practically all of the initial buildings on the Mt. Pleasant Indian Industrial School grounds, the Commercial Block at the northwest corner of Main and Broadway, and the Exchange Bank building at the southeast corner of Main and Broadway. Additionally, Hidey was the contractor/builder for the residences of Dr. Richmond, *see 109 West Locust*, see pages 217-218 and H. E. Chatterton early in his career.

Hidey, who died in 1941 at 84 years old, was preceded in death by his wife Anna in 1938. Together they raised sons Robert and Ralph here. Current city directories show no members of the Hidey family in the area. Subsequent owners include attorney Ray D. Markel, handyman Harry F Chamberlain and his wife Bertha. Since 1959, ownership has resided with members of the Harry F. Chamberlain family and descendants.

619 South University was built in 1895 by Mt. Pleasant attorney Francis H. Dodds, *below in 1906*, and his wife Harriett. Born in Lawrence County, New York, Francis H. Dodds was eight years old when his parents moved to a Coe Township, Isabella County farm. He graduated in the law department of University of Michigan in 1880 and Olivet College in 1882. After a year with Griffith and Dickinson in Detroit, then practiced law in Bay City until 1886, when he came to Mt. Pleasant to enter a partnership with his brother, *see 515 South Main.* In 1893, Peter F. Dodds was elected Circuit Judge and Francis H. continued the practice alone, with offices in the Commercial Building at 128 East Broadway.

He practiced at the Commercial Building address until a sudden heart attack at the family home brought his passing two days before Christmas of 1940. Funeral services were held at the home. Harriet preceded him in death in 1932. Here Francis H. and Harriet Dodds raised Nuget, Daphne, and two other daughters identified in his obituary as Mrs. Buchanan and Mrs. Ben Lewis.

Daphne sold the house in 1952 to postal clerk Lionel P. Haight and his wife Merle, who sold in 1953 to LaVerne Curry, head of the Biology Department of Central Michigan College, and his wife Catherine. Here the Curry's raised Kenneth, Cathy, Cindy, Jane, Matthew.

Since 1978, Kenneth and Aprail Curry have owned the house.

701 South University, right in 1906. This classic Queen Anne house is typified by steeply pitched, irregular roof shapes with a dominant front-facing gable was built in 1905 by building contractor Lewis D. Cole, *below*, of Cole Brothers contracting. The Cole brothers built many of the buildings at the Mt. Pleasant Indian Industrial Schools, the Mt. Pleasant Library. His home was a showcase of his skill, which has stood the test of time, little changed externally to the present.

Lewis D. Cole was born in Lincoln Township, Michigan, and, except, for a year in Sault Ste. Marie, lived here all his life. He and wife Alice, also of Lincoln Township resided in Shepherd until building this home. Here they lived with sons Leo R., Lyle S. , J. Lloyd and Reuel G. Reuel Cole would eventually become longtime owner of Coles Campus Central, buying the complex from Harry Gover, *see 1088 South University, see page 200.*

Isaac A. Fancher, in his 1911 book *Isabella County: Past and Present*, said of the home "It has every modern convenience, is elegantly furnished and neatly kept and the lawn is a thing of beauty."

Lewis D. Cole died at 42 years old July 25, 1910, when he lost control of his automobile near Alma while on his way to Croswell, Michigan, where his company was erecting a new building. His body was found early morning beside the overturned auto. Alice Cole lived in this house until her 1953 death at 85 years old. At her funeral, the family distributed copies of the two page eulogy Isaac Fancher had written in his 1910 book.

In 1961, the Cole family sold the house to Jack and Martha Marken, who sold in 1964 to Maynard and Arline Wielenga. In 1975, the home was sold to another prominent Mt. Pleasant contractor Paul Heydenberg and his wife Carole who sold in 2000 to Craig and Victoria Battle.

The Battles sold in 2009 to Ronald and Theresa Osbourne.

702 South University, left in 1906 The exterior of the house has changed little since Howard E. Chatterton built it in 1904 on the corner where Normal meets Cherry Street. Howard was the son in Chatterton & Son, a company that started as grocers in 1900, then bought the Horning elevator at the northwest corner of Main and Lincoln and became the town's most extensive handlers of grain, hay, wool, potatoes and apples. The house, was the home of Mrs. T. U. Fuller in the 1940s, and was Beacon House, an Isabella County home for wayward children until the county disposed of it in 1976 to Harry and Shirley Klein. Returned to a single family residence, after a succession of owners, Robert C. and Tyler J. Thompson sold the home to Jeffrey S. McDowell and Cameron D. Lewis in 2003.

704 South University, right in 1906, below in 2012 Rising three stories above its two story neighbors, this home was built by Fred F. L. Keeler, for his mother, wife and two children. Keeler was appointed to the Central Michigan Normal School faculty in 1895 as an instructor and head of the Department of Science. In 1908, Keeler left Central to become Deputy Superintendent of Public Instruction at Lansing. In 1913, he was appointed Michigan Superintendent of Public Instruction. Keeler Union, now Powers Hall, on the Central campus, was named for Professor Keeler in 1939.Sometime in the 1930s, the third floor was decimated by fire. Subsequent owners included: auto dealer Art Savage and his wife Violet; Ray F. Cline, founder of Ray F. Cline Advertising and Clinemark at 209 West Broadway, his wife Barbara and son Stephen R. Cline; James and Shirley Carroll; Stephen and Robin Stressman; and, in 2003, Edward Wentworth, Jr. and his wife Deborah.

708 South University was built in 1900 by George Loomis and shortly thereafter was sold to Lucy A. Sloan, who had taught at Kentucky's Berea College and in Lansing city schools before coming to Mt. Pleasant to be Central Normal's preceptress in 1897. Later she would head the English Department at Central, author a textbook, become a popular public speaker and form Central's first literary society. Lucy Sloan died in 1918. In 1941, Sloan Hall opened on Central's Mt. Pleasant campus to house 148 women students on the second floor while a 20-bed health services facility was located in the southern part of the ground floor.

In 1939, the Sloan estate sold the home to C. Willard and Agnes Campbell. In 1960, the house sold to building contractor Richard B. Wood and his wife Sandra. Here they raised son Bruce and daughter Valerie. The photos below chronicle the removal of the large blue spruce in their yard, Woods' donation to the City of Mt. Pleasant, to be used as the City's 1965 Christmas tree at the corner of College (University) and Broadway streets downtown. Although living elsewhere, the Woods retain ownership of the home.

801 South University was built in 1900 by Albert W. Bahlke and his wife Eva. In 1908, the Bahlkes sold to Ward L. Moyer and his wife Minnie. Ward L. Moyer was born in 1874 in Eaton County, Michigan, and married Minnie Clark of Mt. Pleasant in 1901. Together they raised daughters Marjorie and Edith here. For many years, Moyer was an employee of Mt. Pleasant Hardware and Furniture Company and, later, with Kane Hardware and Furniture. Ward l. Moyer died in 1952 and Minnie in 1970, while living at *619 Pine Street.*

From 1925 until 1946, the house belonged to Mrs. Dottie Davidson, who sold in 1946 to Mrs. Mae C. MacDonald, widow of Alexander A. MacDonald, formerly of *419 South University*, and their sons Jack, Donald and William.

In 1954, Mrs. MacDonald rented the house to Central Michigan College Mathematics Professor Harold W. Zeoli and his wife Dorothy. By day, he taught mathematics, but by night Harold was a radio host of an evening mellow music program on the fledgling hometown Mt. Pleasant radio station WCEN. His trademark was the seagulls call opening of the tune "Ebb Tide", a salute to his native Cape Cod, Massachusetts. Here the Zeolis raised twins Carol and Janice, Susan, Stephen and Kristin. After both their demise, the Harold and Dorothy Zeoli's Trust sold the house to William S. and William L. Couchman in 2000, who sold it in 2010 to Tim and Lori Driessnack.

803 South University was Normal Avenue when this Colonial-style home was built by Kendall Page Brooks in 1910. The front elevation is a direct copy of the original home of Governor Bradford of colonial fame, who was a lineal ancestor of Kendall Brooks, whose family originally came from New England.

It was in this house on February 22, 1912, that Kendall's wife and her live-in mother Cynthia M. Page Brooks, Gratia and opened their home to a group of ladies interested in forming a local chapter of the Daughters of the American Revolution, which resulted the organization, of the Daughters of the American Revolution of Isabella County celebrating 100 years in 2012. Mrs. Brooks was also lauded in the Fall 1942 edition of *Centralight* for being a patroness of Alpha Sigma Tau Sorority. ".... and many the college girl who cherishes memories of happy, congenial gatherings in the home."

Born in Kalamazoo, Michigan, where his Baptist minister father was president of Kalamazoo College, Kendall P. Brooks was superintendent of Marquette, Michigan, schools before resigning in 1908 to spend two years studying physics in Germany. He came to Central in 1910 to head the Physics and Chemistry Department. Brooks was also Registrar of the school and the director of Mount Pleasant's Exchange Savings Bank during the Great Depression. For four decades, Brooks served under Central Presidents Grawn, Warriner, and Anspaugh, playing an important part in formatting and establishing policies.

During his tenure, Central grew from a 250 student two-year Normal School to a 3,500 student college offering both baccalaureate degrees and graduate work in the field of education.

Kendall P. Brooks Hall at Central Michigan University became headquarters for the Biology, Chemistry and Physics, Mathematics and Physical Sciences Departments when those moved from Grawn Hall and the Business Department moved to Grawn.

Opened in 1963, Brooks Hall was the largest building on the Central Michigan University Campus, the first classroom building completed since Rowe Hall in 1958. The hall was remodeled in 1970 with help from a Herbert and Grace Dow Foundation grant.

Following his 1964 death and her 1969 passing, the house was sold to Earl R. Nitschke, a Central Michigan University professor, and his wife Laura, who raised sons Kurt and Karl there. In 2008, Nitschke designed the official logo of the Isabella County Sesquicentennial 1859-2009 celebration.

Later owners have included C. Brickner and John F. Nelson and his wife Catherine (Collin) Nelson.

807 South University, left, was built in 1896 by John A. Kennedy and his wife Mary, who sold the house in 1908 to Earnest E. Burdick and his wife Orion, who had it until 1919 when it was sold to Oliver and Emma Troutman, who had it until 1957. From 1957 until 1966, the house was home to banker Gaylord Courter and his wife Marilyn The house was sold in 1968 to CMU Professor Henry L. Fulton and his wife Nancy.

808 South University, above, was built in 1895 by Albert And Eva Bahlke. From 1920 to 1926 the house was owned by John and Ellen Walsh and from 1926 to 1934 it was home to James and Ann Fitzgerald.

In 1934 it was sold to Probate Judge Walter Horn, *left*, and his wife Bernice. Leonard A. Klunzinger of Roosevelt Oil Company and his wife Louise G., bought the home in 1947. Here they would raise sons Bill, Charles, Paul, and Gary, as well as daughter Linda.

The Klunzingers sold in 1998.

1012 South University was Normal Street when this home was built in 1903 by Alexander Burk, family on the porch in this early photograph, *above.* Later the street would become College Street and finally University. Burk died in 1918 and his son William A. Burk sold the house to Andrew Harvey in 1921.

Longtime Mt. Pleasant merchant Noel D. Gover, who had opened his first local store downtown in 1919, and his wife Laura bought the house in 1925. Here they would raise daughters Mary and Helen, as well as sons William, Sheridan, Dwight, Stanley, David and Robert. In 1974, the Gover estate assigned ownership of the home to Michigan Christian Campus Ministry.

1019 South University, below right, was built in 1905 under the ownership of Mary Harvey, whose estate sold the house in 1934 to Walter, Mabel and Harriet Maxwell, who used it as a rental property. Over the years, renters included decorator Henry J. McLaughlin and his wife Lila; tooldresser Harold E. Downhour and his wife Florence; Mt. Pleasant High School teacher Max T. Yeley and his wife Rosalee. In 1963, a parade of one and two year owners began, culminating in 1985 with sale to Charles and Doris Sherwood.

1020 South University, below, was built around 1900 by Charles and Alma Eaton, who sold to William A. McRae and his wife Anastasia in 1903, who in turn sold to Eva Mac Arthur, who lived there six years and sold to Jesse Rowlander in 1919.

In 1921, Charles J. and Amelia A Meyers bought the home and it would remain in the Meyers family through their son petroleum landman Louis J. Meyers and his wife Matilda and then their son John F. "Ace" Meyers, also a petroleum landman until his 1986 death.

From 1986 until 2000 the home belonged to Michael and Deborah Poof, who assigned ownership to MD Inv. Land in 2000.

1088 South University, in the trees boxed by white square left of center below In this 1902 view down Church Street *(later Normal, then College, now University)* the brand new Central Normal Training School, stands just to the right of center, present location of Smith Hall, and beyond that the square building almost dead center of the photo is Zwergels, a campus supply store across the street, in the white square, 1088 South University lies hidden in the trees.

Built about 1892, the same year Central Michigan Normal School and Business Institute opened on 11 acres at the south terminus of Church Street, the house was built by Erwin R. Morrison and his wife Ella. In 1900, it was sold to Icem and Dennis Slentz.

Harry George Gover and his wife Blanche bought 1088 and the business across the street. Zwergels became Gover's Campus Bookstore, adding sporting goods later. Gover also started the Pickwick Office Supply Store with Harry Bentley at 113 East Michigan, later at 122 South University. Harry would operate the Campus Book Store until 1952, when he sold to Reuel Cole and the store became Cole's Campus Store. Harry, *right with sign*, was President of the Mt. Pleasant Chamber of Commerce and helped organize the Michigan Oil and Gas Exposition at Island Park in 1935 that drew more than 25,000 people to town. Harry and Blanche had two daughters, Donna and Ruth. Harry died in 1981, preceded in death by Blanche and Ruth.

In 1985, Donna Gover Brown sold the house to Central Michigan University's Tom Weirich, who sold to Samuel and Salan Haddad in 1998.

The Haddads razed the house and built The Malt Shop in its place.

122 South Washington, right This house was built about 1875 by Fordyce W. Carr and his wife Vianna, who sold in 1926 to John F. and Lillian M Hackett, who sold in the late 1920s to Norman Prior and his wife Thelma, who built on and opened Prior's Service Station here. The Priors raised daughter Rose Marie here.

In the early 1960s, Leon L. Dell and his wife Lois occupied the property and operated Dell's Service Station until the mid-1970s when the property was rented by Lawrence R. and William A. Sheppard, who operated Shepp's Tire Service. Lawrence died in 1953 and William in 1984. In 1985, Thelma Prior sold the property to James and Lois Sheppard. In 2006, the property was sold to Curt and Katherine Ritchey, who operate Curt's Service Center, Inc. auto repair from there.

204 South Washington, below Built by Stephen E. Parrish, who owned the property from 1879 to 1897, the house belonged to Johnson Motor Sales, 202 South College/ University, founder Floyd N. Johnson and his wife Bessie from 1926 until 1939.

From 1939 until 1992, the house belonged to barber Clifford Luce and his wife Opal. Clifford ran Luce's Barber shop from the location, while Opal managed the rooming house portion of the stucture, even after Clifford's mid-1970s death. *Right* is a 1940s snow removal photo with the house visible in the right upper part of the picture.

In 1992, Opal sold the property to David Duba.

214 South Washington, left, was built by wholesale and retail, 130 South Main Street, merchant Stephen Dondero and his wife Kate in 1901. Ownership of the home and the business remained in the family with son Roy and his wife Clare until 1955. Leonard Refineries chemist Lyle A. Pitts and his teacher wife Grace bought the home in1955 and lived there until the late 1970s, when it was purchased by Kevin Abbey and his wife Georgia, who lived there with daughter Emmallia. In 1985, CMU Music instructor Elizabeth Brown bought the house and conveted it to a retail establishment, The Dondero House gift store. In 2001, retailer Tina Hamblin bought it and in 2003 John W. and Judy Parrott turned it over to The Young Church. In 2009, the house became home to the Aphrodite Salon and Boutique.

218 South Washington, right Built in the 1880s, probably by property owner Mary Shaw, this house was owned from 1930 to 1951 by Cletus "Bill" Murray, *below,* in 1943, and his teacher wife Mary Veronica. Here they raised son Grant. In 1951, the house sold to Harry F. Chamberlain and his wife Bertha, parents of Dr. Ray Chamberlain among others. The Chamberlains sold to CMU housekeeper Alice Paisley in 1967. In 1988, until 1999, the house was owned by Lor Nay Sieng, who operated Nay's Bamboo Kitchen and take-out Asian food establishment. In 1999, the house was bought by Pamela Jo Kutchey Dobson, who sold in 2002 to Fitzgerald Properties. In 2006, it became Addiction Solutions and in 2011 Bonnie's Place, with a façade sign reading "ASCC Therapy Solutions."

304 South Washington is an asymmetrically shaped cross-gable Stick style clapboard house on a stone foundation.

The house was built in 1888 by Frank A. Sweeney and his wife Marie. Frank A. Sweeney came to Michigan in 1868 from his native Canada and found work as a stave manufacturer and later a surveyor of timber lands in Saginaw and Bay counties. He came to Isabella County on foot to secure land and timber in 1873, bought a house in Salt River, now Shepherd, to come the rest of the way to Mt. Pleasant. He moved to Mt. Pleasant in 1881 and opened a mercantile store at 114 South Main where he sold groceries and produce, later opening Sweeney Seed Company, Mt. Pleasant's oldest business, with his son Frank J. Sweeney. Here Frank and Marie raised Frank J., Joseph A., Blanid, Rose, Clores, Kathleen Mary Ellen and Eva.

Following the death of Frank A. in 1932 and Marie in 1950, their son, dentist Doctor Joseph A. Sweeney and his wife Elizabeth lived here. Dr. Joseph A. Sweeney graduated the University of Michigan, School of Dentistry in 1927 and practiced in East Detroit, where he married his dental assistant Elizabeth Pohler in 1950. They moved to Mt. Pleasant in 1949 and here raised one daughter, Mary Ellen (Brandell), and four sons, Patrick, Joe, Tom and Jim. "Dr. Joe" Sweeney died in 1964 and Elizabeth followed in 2009.

The house remains under the ownership of Frank A. Sweeney's descendants and is the oldest home in Mt. Pleasant still under the ownership of the family that built it.

404 South Washington above in 1899 was built that same year by 29 year-old dentist Dr. Charles B. Southwick and his wife Nellie. Charles was born in in Kalamazoo, Michigan in 1870 and came to Mt. Pleasant with his family in 1884.

A graduate of Cleary Business College in Ypsilanti, he received his D.D.S. from University of Michigan. After U. of M. graduation, he set up his dentistry practice at 124 East Broadway, which he operated until 1939. The couple was childless and his wife died in 1933.

Dr. Charles B. Southwick

Following Charles Southwick's December, 1957 death at 87 years old, the house, below in 1958, was sold to Northern Supply Company salesman Harold Fox and his wife Vada. Here they raised Barbara, Richard, William, Joseph, and John.

Harold Fox died in 1970 and in 1976 the house was sold to Carol F. Larimer.

In 2012, the house is being painted purple and surrounded by bushes so that no meaningful photograph of the facade is possible.

421 South Washington This home was built in 1882 by William Marlow and sold in 1895 to Tobias and Isabella Bergey. The Bergeys sold in 1906 to Walter E. Carpenter, who sold to George and Sarah Snyder, who in turn sold it to Jay and Lena Servoss.

In 1937, the home was purchased by cattle buyer Loyd Honeywell and his wife Fannie. Loyd Honeywell was born in Lakeview, Michigan, but lived in Mt. Pleasant for 55 of his 71 years of life. Honeywell had a horse barn behind the house that still stands. He was a meat cutter when he was young, starting out with Dan and Emory Johnson and eventually opening his own small grocery store and meat market Honey's Hunk and Chunk at 316 North Mission, later to become Vic Erler's Vic's Super Market when, Floyd retired in 1946. Loyd and Fannie's children were Minnie Honeywell-Bristol, and Melvin "Dutch", in addition to his wife's orphaned niece Virginia Kemmis-Jackson, In 1947, meat cutter Melvin Honeywell bought Carl and Esther Huber's grocery store at 712 South Mission and renamed it Honeywell's, so the name lived on long after Loyd's 1956 death.

In 1947, the Honeywells sold this house to Anna Perry and moved to *1022 East Chippewa.* Anna Perry sold to George Marks in 1966 and the house became a student rental, owned later by Patrick Henry and Nancy McGuirk from 1974 to 2005, when the Nancy J. McGuirk Trust sold it to Quality Apartments.

429 South Washington was built in 1924 by Jacob and Ruth B, Neff, raising Nellie A. and Walter here. The Neff family retained interest in the property until 1979.

In the 1920s, the Neff daughter Nellie and her husband Myron E. Elmore occupied the home. Myron Elmore was born in Isabella County and was a lifelong resident. After graduating from Mt. Pleasant High School in 1909, he attended Central Michigan Normal School where he was considered one of the best catchers and hitters in Central's baseball history. After graduating college, Elmore played semi-professional ball before moving to Seattle where he taught school and had a painting business. In Seattle he joined the U. S. Army during World War I, serving in France and Germany. Following the war he moved back to Mt. Pleasant and started a painting contracting business. In 1938, Elmore started a retail paint store with his son Stanley H. Elmore, which grew into Elmore's Inc., a floor covering, furniture and appliance store. Myron Elmore died in 1964. The Elmore's moved to *741 West High Street* in the early 1950s and the house was rented to C. Floyd Smale of Smale Chevrolet, 706 East Broadway, who moved to *905 Glen.* In the 1960s, the house was rented by Golden Maid Doughnut Shop owner, William E. Golden and his wife Winifred.

The last Neff to occupy the home was teacher John W. Neff and his X-ray technician wife Bonnie, who sold the house in 1979 to Shirley Ann Lord, who sold in 1987 to William David and Kaye B. Pelham.

The Pelhams sold in 1989 to Ivy N. Goduka.

517 South Washington Although records show the house was built in 1894, the owner of the property at the time was Michael Devereaux, whose home was directly behind this location to the east, at *516 South Main.* More likely builders were insurance man Robert Wardrop and his wife Elizabeth, who bought the property in 1919 from property brokers Glen and Grace Riley, who purchased it from the Devereaux estate in 1915. The Wardrops lived in Fowler, MI Elizabeth's hometown, and later in Colorado before moving to Mt. Pleasant in about 1900 to establish what was to become Wardrop & Son insurance, real estate and bonds business with only son Malcomb, see *215 East Chippewa, page 83.* Malcomb continued the business after his father's 1950 and his mother's 1951 deaths.

Independent oil and natural gas explorer-producer John J. Neyer, and his wife Kathleen bought the house, which sits on two lots and boasts a large landscaped yard and garden to the south, in 1951. John came from Beal City MI. In 1928 he had traveled to North Dakota to work in the wheat fields, then worked at the Durant plant in Lansing. In the early 1930s he owned a cattle trucking business, later acquiring two dry cleaning businesses and several gasoline filling stations. He then got in the oil and gas exploration and production business, where he would remain until 1970s retirement. Here they would raise sons Jack, Robert, Kenneth, along with daughters Rose Marie, Patty and Jane.

When the Neyers built a new home on Watson Road in 1967, their daughter Rose Marie and her husband Jerry B. McFarlane bought the South Washington home. In 1976, the house sold to CMU professor Forrest F. Robinson and his wife Linda. Since co-owner 1998, the house has been home to Brass Café and Market on Main Street Susan P. Paton, an avid student of Mt. Pleasant history.

618 South Washington, above, was built in 1890 by Jesse and J. A. Pettit, then sold to: Joseph and Mary Myka in 1909; Albert and Salome Puchart in 1912; and Lester and Anna B. Elder in 1943.

Gravel screener Reuben Hine and his wife Ellen bought the house in 1944 and here they raised Irvin C., Virginia A. and Gerald G. In 1968, the house sold to Susanna Klein and Ford McBride and in 1980, ownership was assigned to Susanna and William Gepford.

630 South Washington, below, is a close architectural cousin to the house at the top of the page with slight modifications. Built by John F. and Clare B. Butcher in 1897, it sold in 1907 to Edward and Edith A. Waldron, who in turn sold in 1916 to Jerry and Sarah Horn. In 1931, Clyde Snelenberger and his wife Clara bought the house and sold it in 1941 to oilman Walter A. Heintz and his wife Mary. The next owners were Fabiano Beverage Company salesman Thomas Tuma and his wife Nell, who worked at Downtown Drugs. The Tumas sold in 1997 to Dorothy A. Archhambeau and Shane McKeoun, who received the 2001 Mt. Pleasant Community Improvement Award. In 2009, the house sold to Ramon Beaulieu.

709 South Washington was built in 1922 by Walter A. and Emma Sneary, who sold it to Benjamin H. and Eunice Demarest in 1923.

The Demarests sold in 1926 to banker J. Elmer and Hannah Elizabeth Graham. J. Elmer Graham, *right in 1943*, was born in 1898 into a banking family. Although he was raised in Gilmore Township, then Farwell, J. Elmer was born in Manitoba, Canada and moved with his family to the U.S. in 1900. His father, Charles, served on the Board of Directors of Farwell Bank. Elmer "filled in" at his brother Allen's position as a teller and bookkeeper at Farwell Bank while Allen served in the U. S. Army during World War I. When Allen came home, Elmer joined Isabella County State Bank as a bookkeeper and teller in 1919, Allen continued at Farwell Bank until 1961 retirement. Another brother, Jesse, was with Shepherd Bank for many years.

Elmer's first promotion at Isabella County State Bank came in 1922 when he was appointed Assistant Cashier. He held that post until 1949, when he was made Cashier. He became Executive Vice President in 1960 and President in 1962. During his career at the bank, one of J. Elmer's major accomplishments was formation of the four-bank computer group in 1964, a bold and innovative move for the day. He retired in 1972, shortly after the bank changed names to Isabella Bank and Trust. Here the Grahams raised sons Pearson and Gordon. J. Elmer Graham died in 1976 and Hannah followed in 1985.

The house was then sold to Alan L. and Barbara J. Emery, who sold it in 2000 to the Shirley Rosen Trust.

802 South Washington On a slight rise overlooking the intersection of Washington and High Streets from the southwest corner, this sprawling wood frame home with wraparound port on the north and east sides oversees the West M-20 "trench" as the highway begins the drop to the bridge on the Chippewa River. The "trench" was dug in the late 1930s to extend High Street to the west side and to allow the rerouting of M-20 away from the downtown area.

The house was built in 1895 by Daniel Anderson and his wife Annie. In 1912, it sold to real estate man Glen H. Riley and his wife Grace, who sold to Milton Bush in 1917.

Mt. Pleasant Lumber Company co-founder George Bugbee, *right,* and his wife Elizabeth bought the home in 1918. Here they raised three sons, Herbert, Wilbur and Russell and four daughters, whose married names are listed in George Bugbee's 1943 obituary as Mrs. W. F. Sowle, Mrs. Ed Cote, Mrs. J. R. Kelley and Mrs. A. H. Zufelt.

The next owner was oilman Carl E. Weller and his wife Lenora T. Here they would raise their family, including Carl E. Junior, DeAnn L. and Nancy L. The Weller family would own the home until 1964, when a series of sales began of the property, used primarily for CMU student rentals, with the latest of those transactions occurring in 1996 when it was sold by Frito Development to Central Michigan Development.

1021 South Washington A cobblestone chimney and flagstone "wainscoting" on the lower front, gives this house a charm like an architectural oasis in a desert of cookie cutter square apartments and dorms abutting the CMU Mt. Pleasant campus. The house reflects the uniqueness of its builder, Frank E. Robinson who built it in 1934 with his wife Laura, Chaplain for the Woman's Relief Corps, *below*, admiring a portrait of Frank for the dedication of the Frank E. Robinson Residence Hall. The Robinsons continued to live behind this house in their home since 1904 at *1068 South Main, now Sigma Kappa house*, using this Washington Street home as a student rental.

Frank E. Robinson never graduated from high school, but passed his teaching examination at Ferris Institute in Big Rapids MI. He attended Central from 1903 to 1905 and earned his life teaching certificate, then his master of arts degree at University of Michigan and taught in Bronson MI, before returning to Central as a teacher in 1911. He headed Central's Department of Commerce from 1916 until State required retirement in 1948 at age 70.

In 1958, the Robinson estate completed sale of the house to then Michigan Consolidated Gas Company Mt. Pleasant Manager John V. Rodenbeck, and his wife Judith, together they raised sons Jack and Peter here. In the mid-1960s, Gerald B. Fuller and his wife Catherine bought the home and lived there until 1975, when it sold to David B. Shirley and his wife Paula E. who owned it until 2000. In 2000, it was bought by William Bennett and in 2010 by Ames LLC and is now a rental unit of Jackel Properties.

(West of Main to Oak)

West: Cherry, Gaylord, High, Illinois, Locust, Maple, Michigan and Wisconsin Streets

209 West Cherry was built in 1894 and was variously home to: Henry and Sarah Patterson; Faula and Mable Bunker; geologist Raymond Hunt and his wife Lois; C. W. Barnhart; retired A & P Manager Norm E. Dawson; Ellen Colthorp, later Elsie Saumier; teacher Linsey Morris; and James Willis. In 2006, Vernon Lee and Carole A. Kennent sold the multiple rental to the Alberta McBride Trust.

219 West Cherry was built in 1894 and the longtime home of the Hills, first engineer Frank S. Hill, then electrician and mechanic Bert J. Hill through the 1920s to 1963, when the house was sold to City of Mt. Pleasant sewage plant superintendent Cornealious Fuller and his wife Lois, a kitchen helper at Mt. Pleasant High School. Since 1994 the rental property has belonged to David Duba.

301 West Cherry In 1894 William Bamber sold this property to Glen H. Riley who built this imposing edifice and lived there until 1911. In 1915, the house was bought by druggist Charles E. Smith, partner with his brother in Mt. Pleasant Drug Store at 201 South Main. The Smith family has owned the house for most of the time since, last occupant being Bernard "Buster" Smith. The house is now vacant.

331 West Cherry was built in 1894, and was home for many years to Ann Arbor Railroad foreman Herbert J. Porterfield and his wife Mable from the 1910s through the early 1950s, when it became home for painter Frederick Wiezork and his wife Gertrude. Currently it is a two apartment rental.

107 West Gaylord was built in 1919 by Eudelmer Willie and his wife Emma, who sold in 1939 to Anna O'Brien, whose estate sold in 1945 to longtime resident Mary Freeman.

In 1951, the house was sold to oilman Stuart A. Merrill, *below*, of Merrill Drilling Company, and his wife Helen. Here they raised Sharon, Glenda, Caroline, Sara, Wesley and Katherine

Born in 1915, Stuart was nine years old when the discovery of oil in Saginaw put Michigan in the ranks of commercially producing oil states, He was 12 years old when the discovery of the Mt. Pleasant oil field on the Isabella-Midland county line catapulted Mt. Pleasant to national prominence and brought hordes of people and jobs here when the Great Depression put the rest of the country in financial straits. When he graduated high school in 1933, at 18, Stuart started Merrill's Casing Service, an oilfield service company, with his father, from whom he inherited the nickname "Shorty". Thus began a 69-year oilfield career, that would see him later join the ranks of Michigan oil and natural gas explorer/producers.

Through the roller coaster fortunes of the oil and gas industry, Stuart remained the eternal optimist, always anxious to serve his good fortune with family, friends and community. He often sponsored local sports teams and his wallet was always open to a good cause. He served on the Mt. Pleasant City Commission 1962-64 and again in 1977, as well as the Isabella County Board of Commissioners 1975-76.

In 1983, the Merrill's sold the house to Alpha Sigma Tau fraternity. Helen died in 2001 and Stuart followed in 2003.

109 West Illinois Exact building date of this structure is difficult to determine but the early history of the property shows that Ernst G. H. Miessler owned the property in 1869 and in 1871 it was sold to Lyman and Martha Crowley, who sold to Moses Brown in 1872. Brown sold to Isaac and Andrew Templeton in 1876.

Probably the house was built during the Templeton ownership period, since in 1897, the Templeton's sold the property to Dr. Albert Getchell and his wife Ella, *see 304 South Main, page 151*, probably as a rental property. In 1916, the house was sold to Wilber Preston, who died in 1917, whose estate sold to Patrick and Lulu Kenny

Patrick Kenny was born in Ireland in 1860. He came to the Mt. Pleasant area at 20 years old to farm. He married Lulu, who was born in Isabella County, and together they raised one son, Leo, as well as daughters Marie, Kathleen and Althea on the farm before the 1917 move to this house after retirement from farming. Patrick Kenny died in 1940, while rooms in the house were rented to four residents. In 1962, the last year of Lulus life, renters occupying the house included: Dow Chemical chemist Paul Dean and his Coleman schoolteacher wife Janet; Central Michigan University student G. M. Donoghue; Credit Bureau employee Clarence McQueen and his typist wife, Shirley.

In 1963, Lulu Kenny sold the house to Farm Bureau Insurance Agency Manager Robert H. Acker, whose estate sold to Pilot Family Properties, Inc. in 2005.

From the look of the mail boxes and containers waiting for trash pickup in the 2012 photo above, five rental units still occupy the house.

109 West Locust, above, in 1906 Physician Dr. Peter E. Richmond's home was called "one of the neatest of modern residences in the city" when built early in the 1898. Dr. Richmond, *left,* was born in 1846 in Louisville, New York, and began teaching in rural schools there when he was 16. He graduated from the medical school at University of McGill in 1873 and set up practice in Mt. Pleasant shortly afterward, having answered the city's call for physicians. He married Anna Gray here in 1877. Richmond was a member of both the American and Michigan Medical Associations and in 1906 was the Grand Medical Director of the Gold Reserve Life Association, a locally-based fraternal insurance organization. In 1902, Dr. Richmond was the first physician in Mt. Pleasant to get x-ray equipment. Dr. Richmond died in 1910.

Following Anna Richmond's 1913 death, the home was acquired from the estate by Robert T. Kane and his wife Cloris. Kane, Mayor of Mt. Pleasant in 1934 and again in 1946, was a descendant of the brick making Kane brothers who were prominent in Isabella County life from arrival here in 1882. The Kanes bought a number of Mt. Pleasant properties, built homes on them to sell to arriving residents. The mild

yellow "Mt. Pleasant brick" still adorns many Mt. Pleasant dwellings. John T. Kane was a co-owner of Breidenstein and Kane Hardware and Furniture store at 121 East Broadway.

The Kane family would occupy the home until 1971, when it sold to Larry and Janice Reynolds, Central Michigan University students, then professors, who raised daughters Monica and Rachel there.

The home remains a private residence.

Below, the property is completely surrounded by a high cedar hedge, having grown several feet since the top photo was taken in 1990.

220 West Locust was built in 1904 by John W. Bechtel, and then sold to William and Sarah Lethorn in 1913. At some point, the home was divided into two or three apartments because records show in 1936 the home was owned by Alva Rahl and had Wellington Graham as a renter. From the late 1930s until her 1951 death at 75 years old, the house belonged to Mrs. Frances Bitler. Renters included H. H. Westbrook and his wife Arah Jean along with son Jack R., *shown right with Mrs. Bitler on the front porch steps in 1942*, and later, infant James.

Later renters included sugar company foreman Harold W. Hodgins and his wife Eloise; and construction worker John Swetz and his wife Alberta, a saleslady at Glen Oren Department store at 121-127 South Main Street.

Later owners included: Isabella County State Bank's William Childs; Oren's Department Store employee Mrs. Beulah M. Ferris; CMU instructor Richard B. Kline; and Carl D. and Rita Eisenberger.

In 2003, the house was bought by Michael and Jane Klumpp of Klumpp Management LLC.

103 West Maple was built in 1906 by wholesale grocer John A. Kenney, whose business started at 320 ½ West Broadway, later moving to 220 West Michigan Street. John A.'s sons James P. and John R. Kenney took over the business upon John A.'s passing and changed the name of the business to Kenney Brothers Wholesale.

James P. Kenney and his wife Bertha took ownership of the house after John A.'s death and here they raised daughter Mildred. Following the passing of both James and Bertha, Mildred retained ownership of the property.

Occupants of the home through the years were: Sun Oil Superintendent Clarence F. Knowlenberg in the late 1940s; D. O. Clinic's Clifford F. Anderson and his wife Georgia in the 1950s; Clare Michigan Holley Carburetor Tool engineer Conrad Christensen, his wife Alta, and children Connie, Sally and Gregory in the 1960s, and Central Michigan University professor Stephen P. Scherer, his wife Carol L. along with their daughters Cynthia and Tanya in the 1970s.

In 1996, 100 years after her grandfather built the house, Mildred Kenney sold to Michael and Susan Marker.

222 and 224 West Maple Note the elaborated crowns on the hood molded windows on the second floor of this triple side-gabled house which has been accommodated with two entrances as a duplex.

The house was built in 1894 by George and Lizzie Lamb. George Lamb was partner in one of Mt. Pleasant's first lumber mills. The Lambs sold to Almond and Emma Lee in 1900, who sold to C. E. Hagen in 1917. Hagen sold to John and Helen Monahan in 1920, who sold to Alonzo and Sarah Crapo in 1934.

The Alonzo Crapo estate sold to the Crapo Insurance Agency's Robert and Margaret Ann Crapo in 1964. Here the Crapos raised Nanette, Stephanie and Michael, now President of the agency.

In 1964, the house was sold to Alma, Michigan school system teacher Gilbert W. Butcher and his Mt. Pleasant Mary McGuire School teacher Jane., who raised Katy, Mike, Greg, Daniel, David and Ronald here. The Butchers lived in the single family dwelling until 1984., Since 1992, the property has belonged to Gregory Butcher.

Renter occupants of the house through the years were: Roosevelt Oil Company driller William A. Miller and his wife Nora in the late 1930s; dentist William H. Barton, his wife Artrude S. and children Jennie L., Lois S. and William A. in the 1940s; accountant John Dean Eckersley and his wife Betty in the 1950s and Dow employee Donald Howie and his wife Patricia in the 1960s.

The "Far" West Side
(North of High to Pickard – West of the Chippewa River)

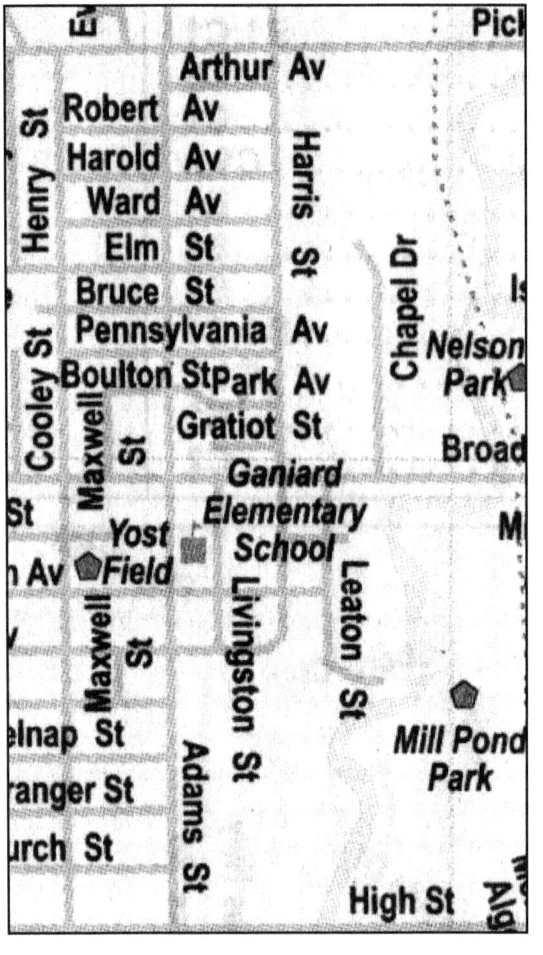

North:
Adams,
Chapel,
Henry.

South:
Adams

West:
Boulton,
Broadway,
Lyons,
Pennsylvania

309 North Adams Probably one of the most dramatic expansion and remodeling jobs performed on a Mt. Pleasant residence has been the transformation of this wood framed home at the southwest corner of Adams and Boulton streets, the finished product shown *above* with before photos of front and rear furnished by the Taylors, *below*.

Isabella County Register of Deeds software's first recording of property ownership shows James and Ida Bacon owning the property in 1928, with City of Mt. Pleasant assessment records indicating the house was built in 1930.

James Bacon died in 1932 and Ida sold the house to Ora B. Taylor in 1932. The property was transferred to Welder Duane G. Taylor and his wife Grace. They took title to the property in 1945 and here they raised a daughter, Betty Lou, and son Gerald. Duane Taylor died in 1980. Grace Taylor, who died in 2004, sold the property to son Gerald and his wife Maureen. The current Taylor residents launched their massive "re-do" in 2010.

1001 North Adams is the last house on North Adams Street on the crest of the hill almost completely surrounded by trees to give both the look and feel of a cottage in the woods. Built in the late 1940s by Martin Holquist, it was the longtime home for the next owners, James A. and Margaret E. Deckard. Both the Deckard's were employed by the Mt. Pleasant State Home and Training School immediately across Pickard street, he in maintenance and she in housekeeping. Here the Deckard's raised son Robert L. "Larry" and Margaret "Cookie".

The Mt. Pleasant Home and Training School was a State of Michigan institution for the mentally challenged on a 320 acre tract of land at the northeast corner of Mt. Pleasant, encompassed by Bamber Road on the west, River Road on the north, Crawford Road (Harris Street in town) on the east and Pickard Street on the south. The institution was the successor to the land which was home to the Mt. Pleasant Indian Industrial School which was a federal industrial boarding school created to acclimate American Indian children with trades and customs enabling them to make a living in the white man's world. The Indian Industrial School operated from 1893 until 1933, when the land was sold to the State of Michigan, leaving a legacy of various attitudes about its existence.

For awhile in the early 1960s, son Larry, an attendant nurse at the Training School and his wife Nancy a CMU student,, along with their children Cathy, Marjorie, and Mary Ann, were the senior Deckard's neighbors at *1111 West Pickard*, prior to moving to Sugarland, Texas, with Dow Chemical Company.

Later owners included: Charles Pumpelly; Eileen Coughlin; Fred and Linda Motz; and Lowell Graham with wife Ann. Longtime 1970s renters were Chippewa Indian Reservation maintenance man Maynard Kahgegab, his wife Ann and their children Camille, Maynard Jr. and Travis.

700, right, and 702 South Adams are architectural identical twins built in the early 1930s to accommodate the population boom brought about by the discovery of the Mt. Pleasant oilfield just before the beginning of the Great Depression of 1929-1939.

Among the first residents of 702 was oilfield rig builder Bill Burden, *below between his two South Adams homes preparing for his 105th birthday in 2012.* When he moved there, arriving from his native Ohio, Burden says, there was no water, sewer, or electric service in 1930, the High Street Bridge crossing the Chippewa River was still eight years away and getting to downtown Mt. Pleasant involved a circuitous route seven blocks south to Broadway Street, the nearest bridge to go east.

He moved away, got married and came back to buy the house at 700 South Adams for $700.00 in 1933. He has lived there ever since. "When we moved here we had a clear view across the millpond and the trains coming through on the other side." Bill says.

Jack-of-all trades, Bill left the oilfields when World War II slowed the oil business to a temporary crawl as men and materials went to the war effort. He was in the construction business for many years, working on such projects as Ganiard School, Barnes and Barnard Halls at Central Michigan College and the Frank Lloyd Wright-designed house and church in nearby Alma, Michigan. He retired more than four decades ago and remains actively enthusiastically pursuing life and his hobbies. Here he and his wife Marie of more than 79 years, raised Donald, Robert, Harry and Elizabeth Ann "Betty".

Later owners of 702 South Adams have included Pleasant Associates; Kimberly Addington; Gerald and Penny LeBlanc; Benjamin, Christopher and Julia Harvey; and Duane and Stephanie Brown.

1206 West Boulton sits on two lots on the north side of a two block street running from one lot east of North Adams Street to two lots west of North Adams. It's legal description puts it in Wards Subdivision, subdivided in 1937 from Boulton's Subdivision, established in 1914, which was a part of Leaton and Upton's Addition to the City of Mt. Pleasant in 1886 on the west side of the Chippewa River.

The house was built in 1937 by Isabella County Highway Department employee Clare Lint and his wife Agnes, who lived here with their son Clyde .

In 1947, the Lints sold the house to welder Floyd and Ann Gill, who lived there with their daughter Betty and son Jack. Floyd began doing welding and minor repair work for hire in the garage at the left, which had front and rear doors to allow "drive through" jobs. This led to the eventual establishment of Gill's Welding Shop at 1956 East Remus Road, the out of city extension of West High Street, a.k.a. West M-20 highway. If that sounds confusing, it's because the east-west numbering dividing line for Isabella County Roads is Meridian Road, some four miles west of the city. Gill's Welding Shop would operate at the Remus Road location for more than five decades.

Ann Gill sold the house to realtor Don Stinson in 1966, who sold it in 1971 to longtime renters Central Michigan University baker Wilhelm Schoenhoff and his Mt. Pleasant State Home and Training School employee wife Elsie E.

The Schoenhoffs sold in 1990 to Craig and Victoria Battle, who sold in 1998 to Leigh and Eva Stanley.

Melissa Largent bought the property from Eva Stanley in 2011.

800 West Broadway/120 North Chapel Drive/, above and upper right in aerial photo, below You aren't likely to find any more residential development on Chapel Drive north of Broadway since this is the entrance road to Riverside Cemetery and for decades has been official, albeit esoteric, address of the attached greenhouse's owners.

In the 1890s, this address belonged to Henry Caple's chicken farm. Around the turn of the 19th Century, Henry changed from chickens to flowers, opening the Mt. Pleasant Greenhouse. Somewhere along the line, a residence was attached to the greenhouse, but not given a Chapel Drive designation until recent years. Later, the business was operated by Walter W. Caple and his wife Maragaret.

In 1945, young Kenneth Elliott came home from World War II and married Caple's daughter, Maxine. Margaret Caple died in 1941 and Walter W. followed in 1945. Ken and Maxine bought the greenhouse, which saw the name changed to Elliott's Greenhouse, a name that's lasted more than five and a half decades at this writing. The Elliott's were prime movers on Mt. Pleasant social and civic scene for many years. Elliot's Greenhouse, Inc. President Paul Elliott, Kenneth and Maxine's son, who lent us the above 1952 picture off his office wall, and now resides at the address.

815 West Broadway According to City of Mt. Pleasant Assessment software, this house was built in 1900 under the ownership of George Wright but it was more likely built by retiree Colin Angus McCall and his wife Adeline when they moved to Mt. Pleasant from Saginaw in 1912. In Saginaw, they had raised a son, John B. McCall, and a daughter Leota (Dexter). Leota died sometime before 1911, when John B. came to Mt. Pleasant, *see 309 East Wisconsin, page 114,* and his parents the following year.

Here the McCalls celebrated their 65th wedding anniversary shortly before Colin died in March of 1945 and Adeline followed in 1953 having survived all of her immediate family *(John B. succumbed in 1952, after having served 33 years as Mt. Pleasants Fire Chief)*. Both funeral services for the elder McCalls were conducted at this house. In 1954, Kenneth and Maxine Elliott, of Elliot's Greenhouse, across the street, bought the house from the McCall's granddaughter Mary Cooper.

Rent-to-own Elliott's Greenhouse grower/florist Lloyd E. Carroll and his florist wife Dorothy occupied the house from 1953 forward, purchasing it in 1967. Here the Carrolls raised Susan, Marilyn, Joseph, David and Michael.

In 2009, the Lloyd E. Carroll estate sold the property to P & K Seybert Holdings LLC, who razed the house and replaced it in 2012 with an addition to the Rivers Bluff Senior Townhomes complex at 805 West Broadway.

819 West Broadway As you drive west on Broadway in the summertime, just as you get to Leaton Street, you'll see this house and usually a guy sitting in the chair by the front door, honk and wave. That's Jack Taylor, retired driver/salesman for Culligan Soft Water Service and father of John, Gale and Deborah. He's owned the place since 1971.

The house was built in 1915 by Wellington J. Beebe, who owned one of Mt. Pleasants earliest automobile repair shops as part of his machine shop at 311 West Broadway. In 1936, the Wellington J. Beebe estate sold the house to Edward and Pearl Harris, who sold in 1944 to Leo and Gladys Whitney.

By 1947, trucker Albert Wood and his wife Marie were owners of the house, where they lived with sons Richard and Robert as well as daughter, Shirley. In 1957, the Woods sold to Ferros Stamping Company tool and die maker Victor J. Merchand and his wife Caroline, who lived there with daughters Annette, Denise and Patricia.

Jack Taylor bought the house from the Merchands in 1971 and after a career of meet and greets with Culligan Soft Water, serves as unofficial greeter to those approaching the west side from the east during the warmer months of the year.

1015-1021 West Broadway - "Back in the day"...as the kids are wont to say, the 1000 block of West Broadway was practically a self-contained settlement of its own for fiercely independent "Far westsiders"....Christopher and Margurite Graham Torpey built their store at **1021 West Broadway** in 1930, and later added living quarters in the back, where Christopher and daughters Virginia and Suzanne are shown with the large back yard in the bottom photo. Down the street, at **1001 West Broadway** was Nagy's gas station, later owned by Lynn *Jones, see below*, and across the street at **1014 to 1018,** Lawrence Tanner had a Shell gasoline filling station, there was a barber shop and later a candy store with a post office substation, as well as Milo J. and Euretta Jones grocery store.

The Joneses raised son Lynn, *see 1111 West Lyons Street*, page 233, and daughter Kay in a house behind their store, which burned in 1975. Milo Jones sold the store at **1108** to Luigi "Louie" Deni in 1966.

Meantime across the street, in 1935, Christopher and Margurite built a house on their property at **1015 West Broadway**, which remains in Torpey family ownership.

1301 West Broadway The house with the big "T" has an indefinite building date but is believed by current resident William Tschappat to have been built around 1917 and was the farmhouse for a 40 acre spread that encompassed the area bounded by Broadway Street on the north, Michigan Street on the south, Henry Street on the west and Adams Street on the east.

In 1935, National *(oilfield)* Supply Mt. Pleasant manager Henry Tschappat, *left,* and his wife Alma bought the house from oil and gas drilling contractor Jim Berneer. Henry Tschappat had joined National Supply Company in his native Ohio following a stint in the U. S. Army during World War I. When the first Michigan oilfield discovery was made at Saginaw in 1925, Henry opened the first oil field supply store in the state at Saginaw in 1926. Later he was assigned to Muskegon and then, when the Mt. Pleasant oilfield developed in 1928, he opened the Mt. Pleasant store for National here in 1931. Highly regarded both as an oil field supply representative and an avid booster of Mt. Pleasant west side development, Henry died in 1948 at 54 years old, having worked for National Supply for 32 years.

Originally from Pennsylvania, Alma Tschappat, *right in 1943 when she was president of the then newly-formed Mt. Pleasant Council of Parent Teacher Associations*, was the school kitchen and community canning center director and an active and formidable civic leader until her 1972 death at 71 years old.

Tschappat offspring raised here were sons Henry Jr., Ella Nora, William and Andrew.

William Tschappat remembers World War II Victory Gardens in the field to the east of the house, where free movies were shown on a huge screen in the late 1940s. He also remembers a barn where he raised chickens and sold eggs for fifteen cents a dozen.

Pictured in 1949 right to left back row. – Lyman "Butch" Mead, Jr. and Jack R. Westbrook; and front row Phillip Mead and James Westbrook; and Dick Mead, right with back to the camera

309 to 312 North Henry (earlier known as 1309 West Pennsylvania) The "more than 60 year old" photo above surfaced recently when the author's childhood, neighborhood friend, Dick Mead, "caught up" over coffee after almost 20 years of no contact after life created divergent paths. The picture was taken around 1949 in the yard of the Mead home at **1305 West Pennsylvania**, occasion unknown, but the relevance to this book is the houses in the background, both replaced by more modern structures. Until the late 1940s, there was no north Henry street so the house on the right was designated **1309 West Pennsylvania** until demolition in the late 1980s and construction of a duplex in 1993*, below*, owned by Kathleen Williams and designated **310-312 North Henry.**

309 North Henry, *left background above*, belonged to Elizabeth Miller when the photo was taken and was probably demolished later. The current structure was built in 1983 by Leo and Rogue Bernard, assigned to Bernard and Marilyn Shafer in 2002, who sold to Christina Alger the same year. Christine Alger sold to Virg and Danielle Phillips in 2009.

310-312 North Henry, *right above*, in 1949 was the "brand new" home of Mt. Pleasant city employee mason tender William Walldorff and his wife Dorothy, parents of Loretta, Leona, Gladys, Donald and Charles. Later in 1949, "Willie" added a bivouac tent, which he later covered with tar paper and continued to add room additions to the structure until his 1974 death. Dorothy died in 1962.

What the west-siders jokingly dubbed the "Walldorff Astoria" was lost to back taxes in 1983. The property acquired by Ms. Williams in 1993, who built the duplex *left*.

1111 West Lyons Earliest Isabella County Register of Deeds records on this property in the Leaton and Lyons Addition to the City of Mt. Pleasant is for the year 1889, probably the year the land was added to the city. Ownership then lay in the hands of George M. Edmonds, who sold to Lowell H. Glover in 1895, who in turn sold the property to Harold and Laura Ohms in 1925, who probably built the house. The next property owners, in 1938 were Standard Oil trucker William and Aletha Grace, who lived here with daughter Janet.

Leo Matthews, *below in a 1943 caricature*, of Murray's Tire Shop later Mt. Pleasant Tire at 420 East Broadway and his wife Alta owned the house from the mid 1940s and lived there with daughters Grace and Opal. The Mathews sold to Norbert and Mary Martin in the mid 1960s, who apparently rented the house since the 1972 Polk's city directory for Mt. Pleasant shows renter Sue Cain, Becky McGowan and Patricia Milkavich living there. In 1974, the property sold to Stanley and Steven Martin, who in turn sold in 1976 to Lynn G. Jones and his wife Veronica Jean, who worked for Enterprise Printers and later for Wal-Mart. Lynn Jones was owner of the Leonard gasoline filling station and auto repair business at 1001 East Broadway and later worked for Mt. Pleasant Plumbing and Heating. Here they raised Jeff, Danny, Jennifer and Scott. Lynn continues to be one of the prime organizers, along with Shirley French, of the West Side Reunion, held in July each year at Mt. Pleasants Island Park.

1011 West Pennsylvania this front dormered classic ranch style home was built in the 1930s and was the longtime home of legendary oilfield welder K. W. "Red" Utterback and his wife Mildred. Born in Six Lakes, Michigan, in 1916, Utterback came to Mt. Pleasant in 1931 when his father was appointed Supervisor of the Michigan Highway Department operation here. At 16 years of age, he got a job with a pipeline crew and loved to tell the story of how he became a welder. "They asked if anybody 'knew how to torch'" Red would say "and I figured that whatever it was it was better than ditch digging so I said 'Yes.' ". Thus began a welding career that would last for 70 years. Here "Red" and Mildred raised daughters Linda and Brenda. Utterback died in 2006, preceded in death by Mildred by two decades.

1103 West Pennsylvania has stayed in the Blizzard family since oilfield worker Bernard Blizzard bought the property from Arthur Ward in 1938 and built this house, later remodeled. Here Bernard and Sue raised Liston, Bernard Jr., Walter, Lewis, Michael, John, Louella and Katherine. Bernard Blizzard died in 1987 and in 1990 Suzie sold the house to son John Blizzard..

Appendix 1

Mt. Pleasant Original Plats and Additions

The following is a compendium of additions the city of Mt. Pleasant with years the Addition was recorded at the City of Mt. Pleasant Assessors Office.

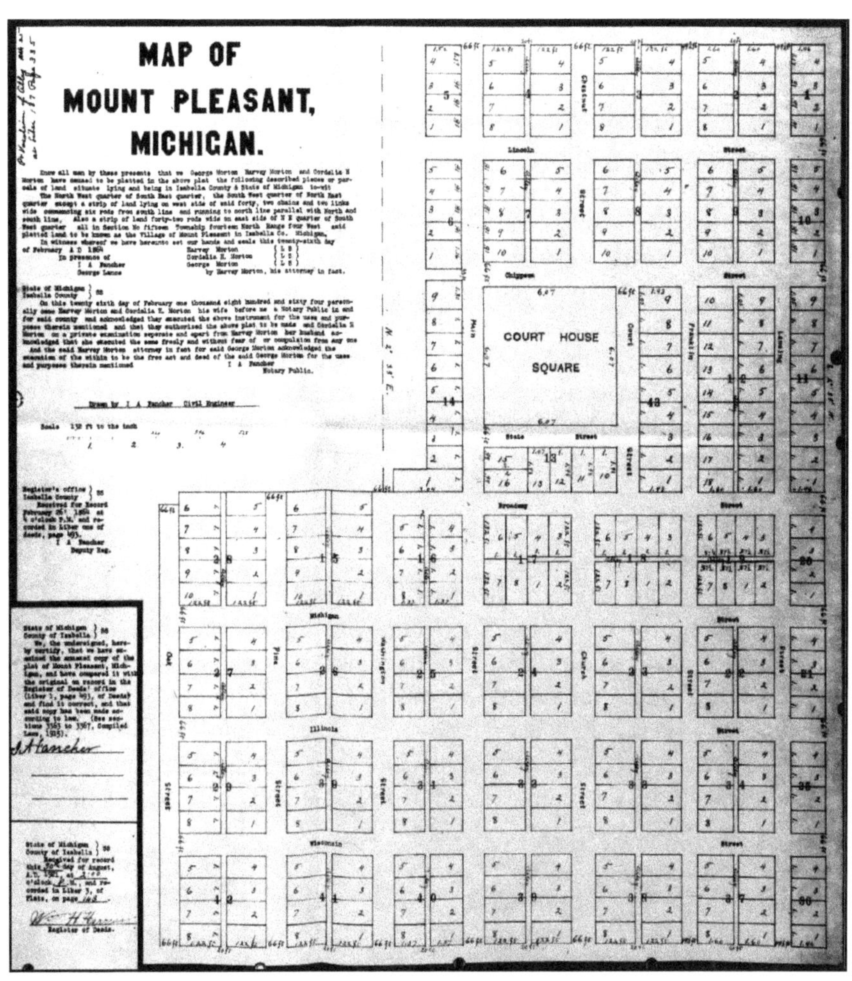

Isaac A. Fancher's 1864 plat of Mt. Pleasant: "The Original Plat"

Mt. Pleasant becomes a place

Lumberman David Ward had timbered off his 200 acre holdings on the high ground beside the Chippewa River beginning in 1856. In 1860, he platted a village and named it Mt. Pleasant because the area reminded him of his boyhood home in Pleasant Valley, and the high banks of the Chippewa River where his land was located was reminiscent of a small mountain. In 1860 Ward gave the new Isabella County government five acres if they would move the county seat to his village, which he then sold to George Morton, a New York investor, George's nephew Harvey Morton and wife Cordelia were sent to promote the new village.

Isaac Fancher was born September 30, 1833, in Montgomery, New York. He was married June 6, 1860, to Althea Preston at Java, New York, shortly after he left law school. After a stint of prospecting for silver in Nevada, the Fanchers returned from the west to Kilbourn City, Wisconsin, where his parents had moved from New York state. Shortly thereafter, his wife received word that her father, Albert Preston, brother Wallace, sister Ellen and her husband Samuel Woodworth, had moved to a tiny settlement in central Michigan named Mt. Pleasant, where Ellen was the first schoolteacher in the newly named Isabella County seat. Probably at the behest of Althea, the young Fancher family moved to Mt. Pleasant.

When 30 year-old Isaac Fancher arrived in Mt. Pleasant on July 4, 1862, there were two houses.

A crude cabin served as the first County Building just south of Mr. Preston's home at the corner of Main and Chippewa streets. Harvey Morton, who was building a hotel at the corner of what is now Main and Broadway to house potential prospective buyers of lots in the new village, sold Isaac Fancher three lots along Main Street. Fancher suggested that a new survey be done since the original plat had not been registered. One of Fancher's first Mt. Pleasant jobs was conducting the first registered plat of the village.

Original Plat – 1864. Lots numberd 00001-00 to 00613-00. The original plat of Mt. Pleasant, prepared by Isaac Fancher to standardize the rough plat of the place sold to the Morton Brothers by David Ward, was registered in 1864. The plat was bordered on the north north of Broadway by five lots north of Lincoln Street,on the west by Main Street, on the east by Lansing Street and on the west south of Broadway by Oak Street . The entire original plat is bounded on the east by Lansing Street on the four lots south of Wiscpnsin Street.south of Broadway

OTHER PLAT ADDITIONS TO THE CITY OF MT. PLEASANT

NAME OF PLAT	YEAR
Original Plat	1864
Hopkins Addition	1875
Smiths Addition	1875
Kinney's Addition	1877
Hall's Addition	1880
Partridge's Addition	1880
C. Bennett's Addition	1882
Fordyce Addition	1884
Kinney's 2nd Addition	1884
Hopkins & Lyon's Addition	1886
Leaton & Upton's Additions	1886
Young & Vedders Addition	1887
Nelson's Addition	1889
Brown & Leaton's Addition	1890
Bamber's Addition	1891
Stones Outlets	1891
Bennett & Burrows	1892
College Hill Addition	1892
Hance's Additions	1892
Normal School Addition	1893
Crowley's Addition	1894
Crowley's Outlots	1894
M. Browns Addition	1895
Martin's Addition	1897
Lea's Addition	1898
Damon Subdivision	1912
Meadow Park Addition	1912
Boulevard Park	1914
Kinney & Richmond's Addition	1914
Yorba Linda Subdivision	1918
Boulton's Subdivision	1919
Burch Subdivision	1919

Dersnah's Addition	1919
Dersnah's Subdivision	1919
Granger Heights	1919
Mission Garden's	1919
Old Town Subdivision	1919
Sunny Side Plat	1919
Transport Heights	1919
Whitney's Addition	1919
Bentley's Addition	1921
Burch's Subdivision	1921
Neal's Subdivision	1935
College Park	1936
Pleasant View	1936
Ward's Subdivision	1937
Ward's View Subdivision	1937
Ward's Addition	1938
Ward's Heights	1939
Ward's Outlots	1939
Moutsatson Subdivision	1941
Glamour Gardens	1943
Victory Gardens	1944
Axtell Terrace No. 1	1946
Bruce View	1946
College Heights	1946
Hutchinsons Subdivision	1946
Pleasant View No. 2	1946
Garden Grove	1947
Landon Subdivision	1947
Lee's Addition	1947
Poulos Subdivision	1947
Samson's Subdivision	1947
South Mission Heights	1947
Axtell-Gorden Addition	1948
Axtell Terrace No. 2	1948
Belmont Park	1948
Burdicks Southview	1948
Campus View	1948

Hoyle's Subdivision	1948
Roger's Heights	1948
Westview	1948
Assessors Plat No. 1	1949
Curtiss Court	1949
Lawrence Heights	1949
Pleasant View No. 3	1949
Southlawn No. 1	1949
Assessors Plat No. 2	1950
Burdicks Southview No. 2	1950
Davis-Leonard Addition	1950
Axtell Acres	1952
Garden Grove No.2	1952
Stockman Acres	1952
Taylor's Addition	1952
Blesh Meadows Subdivision	1953
Carter's Subdivision	1954
Chippewa Village	1954
Dyer's Garden Plat	1954
Cernak's Subdivision	1955
Eastwood	1955
Greenfield Acres	1955
Riverview Subdivision	1955
Assessors Plat No. 3	1956
Assessors Plat No. 4	1956
Broadway Acres	1956
Lynwood Subdivision	1956
O'Hara's Subdivision	1956
Greenbrier Estates	1957
Myers Subdivision	1957
Prospect Park	1957
Solar Heights	1957
Elizabeth Court	1958
Mead's Little Acres Subdivision	1958
Prospect Park Addition	1958
Airport Acres	1959
Day Woods	1959

Dimits Subdivision	1959
Prospect Park No. 3	1959
Riverview Subdivision No. 2	1959
Sansotes Addition	1959
South Gate	1959
Assessors Plat No. 5	1960
Breidenstein Acres	1960
Bruce View No. 2	1960
Smalley's Subdivision	1960
Sunset Subdivision	1960
Veits Subdivision	1960
Assessors Plat No. 6	1961
Broomfield Heights	1961
Riverview Subdivision No. 3	1961
Snyder's Subdivision	1961
South Gate No. 2	1961
Westview No. 2	1961
Wings Subdivision	1961
Wood Meadows	1961
O'Hara's Subdivision No.2	1961
Westchester	1962
Wendrow Estates	1963
Edgewood Subdivision	1963
Beltinck Subdivision	1964
Thomas Subdivision	1964
Holiday Estates	1964
Bamber Woods	1965
Wood Meadows No. 2	1965

Appendix 2
Mt. Pleasant Centennial Homes

Plaques awarded in 1989 during Mt. Pleasant's celebration of the 100th Anniversary of the 1889 designation of the community as a city.

426 South Franklin –. Howard Brownson.

617 East Broadway – Mrs Albert Stangle

1990 Bamber Road – Bill and Marie McCracken

221 North Kinney - Richard Bellinger

510 South Franklin - Joseph and Jennifer McDonald

424 South Kinney - John and Barbara Hunt

108 Oak Street - Norman III and Joan Curtis

315 East Chippewa - Merle E. Aldrich

222 East Wisconsin - Hazen Roy Pittsley

621 North University - John and Barbara Sardo

430 South Lansing - Maxine Tanner

319 South University - Art Reach of Mid –Michigan

503 East Broadway - Charles and Nancy Lux

1917 West Blanchard - Peter and Elizabeth Hanley

501 North Fancher - Jack and Mary Lou Westbrook

4199 South Shepherd - Theresa Myles Conroy

636 South Lansing - Tim and Judy Lannen

415 East Chippewa - Alan and Diane Shinaver
708 South Main - George N. and Ernestine R. Lauer
301 East Chippewa - Margaret Doughty
308 East Andre - Myron and Mary Huggins
321 North Kinney - Jerry Sheahan
206 South University - Dorothy A. Johnson
317 North Fancher - Juliann Pell
315 East Wisconsin - Richard A. Tilman
507 North Lansing - Harold Lentz
314 East Andre - Ethel Connors
Southwest Union Twp. – Stuart Merrill
1691 South Lincoln Road – John McDonald
514 South Main - Mark and David Coyne
933 West Deerfield Road – Robert Butka
614 East Broadway - Reba Dedie
506 North Fancher - James Owen
606 North Fancher - George D. Aultman
309 East Andre - Stanley Pridgeon
311 East Andre - David Andrews
509 South Fancher - Mr. and Mrs. Thomas Minke
309 East Wisconsin - Mr. and Mrs. Steve Way
420 South Franklin - Leo Kipfmueller
512 South University - Alfred L. Neff
109 West Locust - Andy Woodrick
721 North Fancher - S.K. Muszynski
503 North University - Mr. and Mrs. David Massee
312 North Franklin - Don and Susan Fuller
314 North Franklin - Don and Susan Fuller
325 North Fancher - Dwight and Betty Reava
304 South Washington - Elizabeth Sweeney
110 South Washington - Sweeney Seed Company
220 West Michigan - Kenney Brothers Wholesale

Appendix 3
City of Mt. Pleasant Community Improvement Awards

1979

300 East Bellows - Reul Cole, Residential .
222 North Mission - Conrad English, Commerical .

1980

515 North Kinney – Joe & Sheryl Olivieri, Residential .
130 South Main - Marilyn LaBelle, Commerical

1981

304 North Lansing - John Coles, Residential
109 East Broadway - Larry Everts, Commercial
210 Court Street – Dean Eckersly, Commercial

1982

113 North Harris – Dennis & Kimberly Martin, Residential
405 South Mission – LaBelle Management, Commercial
215 South Mission – Cindy's Flower Boutique, Commercial

1983

415 North University – Carol Quillen, Residential
117 South University – Jim Stein, Commercial

1984

721 North Fancher – Sher Muszynski, Residential
615 North Mission – Cook's Music, Commercial
215 West Broadway – Kerr & Campbell, Commercial

1985

514 South Main –David & Mark Coyne (Phi Sigma Sigma) Residential
108 South University – Sid & Judy Smith, Commercial

1986

702 South Main – Robert Neyer, Residential
223 North Mission – Kentucky Fried Chicken, Commercial

1987

304 South Washington – Elizabeth Sweeney, Residential
300 South University – Taylor, Pyscher & O'Neil, Commercial

1988

415 East Chippewa – Alan & Diane Shinaver, Residential
600 Industrial Ave. – Thielen Turf, Commercial

1989

No Awards were made in either division.

1990

422 North Main – Dan & Laurie Powell, Residential
116 Court Street – Paul Alexander, Commercial

1991

221 North Kinney – Patricia Click, Residential
302 North Mission – LaBelle Management, Commercial
121 East Broadway – Bill McCarthy's Downtown Drugs, Commercial

1992

623 South Washington – Richard & Donna Maatman, Residential
125 East Broadway – Max & Emily's Bakery & Café, Commercial

1993

1301 East High – Richard & Donna Parr, Residential
131 South Main – Wakely & Associates, Commercial
106 Court Street –Club Shaboom, Commercial

1994

425 South University –Olivieri Management, Residential
1027 South Franklin –University Coffee Cup, Commercial

1995

908 East High – Shelley & Robert Kemmerling, Residential
509 North Mission – Mt. Pleasant Floor Covering, Commercial

1996

506 North Fancher- John and Susan Blick, Residential
506 East Broadway – Mountain Town Station, Commercial

1997

1403 East Gaylord – Olivieri Management, Residential
1415 East Pickard –Kraphol Ford, Commercial
324 South Mission – Little Caesar's, Commercial

1998

408 South Kinney – Trenton & Kimberly Stange, Residential
1106 West High – River Project, Commercial

1999

401 Pine – Michael & Serenity Brady, Residential
109 Oak (311 West Broadway) – Sam Staples, Commercial

2000

415 East Chippewa – Jack Neyer, Residential
317 North Mission – Family Video, Commercial
711 West Pickard – Commerce Center, Commercial

2001

630 South Washington – Dorothy Archambeau & Shane

McKeown, Residential

215 North Main – Boge, Wybenga & Bradley, Commercial

2002

310 South Fancher – Herbert & Janice Voege, Residential

120 South Fancher – Mt. Pleasant Tire Service, Commercial

2003

715 North Fancher – Mark Weideman, Residential

930 West Broomfield- The Cabin Bar, Commercial

2004

311 North Franklin – Christopher & Rebecca Bundy, Residential

502 West Broadway – Waterworks Salon & Spa, Commercial

2005 & 2006

1414 East Broadway –Eric Curtiss, Residential

1010 East High – Michael & Denise Stockton, Residential

812 Crescent – Daniel & Lora Odykirk, Residential

139 East Broadway – Isabella Bank & Trust, Commercial

1218 South Mission – Scheppe Pie Shops (Grand Traverse Pie Company), Commercial

2007

601 North Kinney –Michael & Marcia Brockman, Residential

106 Court Street – Richard Swindlehurst, Shaboom Pub/Blue Gator, Commercial

2008

No Awards were made in either division.

2009 & 2010

802 South Main – Joseph Olivieri, Residential

1023 & 1025 South Washington – Jeff Jakeway, Residential

1143 South Mission – Bells & Birds for Taco Bell, Commercial

602 Industrial Drive – Michael & Bonnie Zingery, Commercial

1306-1416 South Mission-Bobenal Investments (MC Sports Plaza), Commercial

2011

103 West Maple – Michael & Susan Makker, Residential

1007 South Main – Oliveri Homes, Residential

309 North Main – Jean M. Prout Trust Ginkgo Tree Inn, Commercial

114-116 East Broadway –Jim Goodrich (original J.C. Penny Store), Commercial

Appendix 4 – Early Mt. Pleasant Homes not included in this Volume

The following addresses and dates of construction on file with the City of Mt. Pleasant Assessors Office were photographed and/or researched for this book but are not included. These research materials are available at the Clarke Historical Library in the Park Library building on the Mt. Pleasant, Michigan, campus of Central Michigan University.

#	Direction	Street	Year
211	NORTH	ADAMS	1930
215	NORTH	ADAMS	1925
203	EAST	ANDRE	1880
204	EAST	ANDRE	1936
209	EAST	ANDRE	1983
215	EAST	ANDRE	1890
222	EAST	ANDRE	1884
224	EAST	ANDRE	1909
312	EAST	ANDRE	N/A
412	EAST	ANDRE	1935
509	EAST	ANDRE	1900
510	EAST	ANDRE	1982
606	EAST	ANDRE	1925
621	EAST	ANDRE	1940
120	SOUTH	ARNOLD	1934
209	NORTH	ARNOLD	1936
311	NORTH	ARNOLD	1900
312	SOUTH	ARNOLD	1884
401	SOUTH	ARNOLD	1936
410	SOUTH	ARNOLD	1890
420	SOUTH	ARNOLD	1904
500	NORTH	ARNOLD	1935
502	SOUTH	ARNOLD	1930
516	NORTH	ARNOLD	1900
521	NORTH	ARNOLD	1914
601	SOUTH	ARNOLD	1950

608	NORTH	ARNOLD	1944
609	NORTH	ARNOLD	1884
610	NORTH	ARNOLD	1925
612	NORTH	ARNOLD	1931
615	SOUTH	ARNOLD	1909
710	SOUTH	ARNOLD	1924
807	NORTH	ARNOLD	1900
1005	SOUTH	ARNOLD	1934
1008	SOUTH	ARNOLD	1940
1016	SOUTH	ARNOLD	1946
109	EAST	BENNETT	1890
200	EAST	BENNETT	1945
201	EAST	BENNETT	1934
210	EAST	BENNETT	1904
211	EAST	BENNETT	1934
215	EAST	BENNETT	1900
216	EAST	BENNETT	1900
220	EAST	BENNETT	1879
302	EAST	BENNETT	1924
303	EAST	BENNETT	1900
309	EAST	BENNETT	1900
310	EAST	BENNETT	1904
517	EAST	BENNETT	1947
401	EAST	BROADWAY	N/A
407	EAST	BROADWAY	1894
410	EAST	BROADWAY	N/A
612	EAST	BROADWAY	1946
616	EAST	BROADWAY	N/A
623	EAST	BROADWAY	N/A
624	EAST	BROADWAY	1920
814	WEST	BROADWAY	19036
1002	EAST	BROADWAY	1910
1425	EAST	BROADWAY	1968
211	WEST	CHERRY	1994
215	WEST	CHERRY	1905
303	WEST	CHERRY	1884

309	WEST	CHERRY	1916
314	WEST	CHERRY	1920
318	WEST	CHERRY	1905
322	WEST	CHERRY	1890
325	WEST	CHERRY	1914
406	EAST	CHERRY	1900
410	WEST	CHERRY	1985
411	WEST	CHERRY	1901
213	EAST	CHIPPEWA	N/A
313	EAST	CHIPPEWA	1955
315	EAST	CHIPPEWA	1894
608	EAST	CHIPPEWA	N/A
700	EAST	CHIPPEWA	1937
221	WEST	CLAYTON	1935
805	SOUTH	DOUGLAS	1917
806	SOUTH	DOUGLAS	1925
911	SOUTH	DOUGLAS	1937
115	SOUTH	FANCHER	1914
117	NORTH	FANCHER	1900
117	SOUTH	FANCHER	1905
124	NORTH	FANCHER	1900
201	SOUTH	FANCHER	R2004
204	NORTH	FANCHER	1904
207	NORTH	FANCHER	1920
209	NORTH	FANCHER	1900
310	SOUTH	FANCHER	1884
318	NORTH	FANCHER	1985
322	NORTH	FANCHER	1900
401	SOUTH	FANCHER	1904
402	SOUTH	FANCHER	1988
413	NORTH	FANCHER	1904
420	SOUTH	FANCHER	1912
421	SOUTH	FANCHER	1900
422	NORTH	FANCHER	1904
432	SOUTH	FANCHER	1900
438	SOUTH	FANCHER	1905

439	SOUTH	FANCHER	1900
501	SOUTH	FANCHER	1900
504	SOUTH	FANCHER	1900
509	SOUTH	FANCHER	
510	SOUTH	FANCHER	1900
515	NORTH	FANCHER	1928
518	NORTH	FANCHER	1904
520	SOUTH	FANCHER	1905
523	NORTH	FANCHER	1900
524	SOUTH	FANCHER	1900
602	SOUTH	FANCHER	1900
608	NORTH	FANCHER	N/A
614	SOUTH	FANCHER	1900
619	SOUTH	FANCHER	1938
620	SOUTH	FANCHER	1905
622	NORTH	FANCHER	1900
623	NORTH	FANCHER	1900
630	SOUTH	FANCHER	1912
631	SOUTH	FANCHER	1930
700	SOUTH	FANCHER	1905
704	NORTH	FANCHER	1890
710	SOUTH	FANCHER	1910
717	NORTH	FANCHER	1910
750	SOUTH	FANCHER	1900
801	SOUTH	FANCHER	1919
804	NORTH	FANCHER	1905
804	SOUTH	FANCHER	1939
805	SOUTH	FANCHER	1904
810	NORTH	FANCHER	1900
815	SOUTH	FANCHER	1920
821	NORTH	FANCHER	1919
822	NORTH	FANCHER	1900
901	SOUTH	FANCHER	1864
924	SOUTH	FANCHER	1938
931	SOUTH	FANCHER	1894
1005	SOUTH	FANCHER	1884

1007	SOUTH	FANCHER	1937
1026	SOUTH	FANCHER	1901
1027	SOUTH	FANCHER	1924
1028	SOUTH	FANCHER	1933
1033	SOUTH	FANCHER	1936
1036	SOUTH	FANCHER	1936
1037	SOUTH	FANCHER	1914
1220	NORTH	FANCHER	1920
1608	NORTH	FANCHER	N/A
314	NORTH	FRANKLIN	
426	SOUTH	FRANKLIN	
810	SOUTH	FRANKLIN	N/A
811	SOUTH	FRANKLIN	1905
814	SOUTH	FRANKLIN	1905
820	SOUTH	FRANKLIN	1917
901	SOUTH	FRANKLIN	1890
904	SOUTH	FRANKLIN	1930
905	SOUTH	FRANKLIN	1890
906	SOUTH	FRANKLIN	1905
921	SOUTH	FRANKLIN	1915
925	SOUTH	FRANKLIN	1900
1001	SOUTH	FRANKLIN	2009
1002	SOUTH	FRANKLIN	1900
1005	SOUTH	FRANKLIN	1910
1006	SOUTH	FRANKLIN	1932
1007	SOUTH	FRANKLIN	1920
1010	SOUTH	FRANKLIN	1935
1011	SOUTH	FRANKLIN	1920
1013	SOUTH	FRANKLIN	1900
1015	SOUTH	FRANKLIN	1900
1016	SOUTH	FRANKLIN	1915
1018	SOUTH	FRANKLIN	1900
1021	SOUTH	FRANKLIN	1900
1023	SOUTH	FRANKLIN	1905
1027	SOUTH	FRANKLIN	N/A
1028	SOUTH	FRANKLIN	1900

1031	SOUTH	FRANKLIN	1900
1032	SOUTH	FRANKLIN	1900
1036	SOUTH	FRANKLIN	1900
1023	WEST	GRATIOT	1901
207	EAST	HIGH	1910
215	EAST	HIGH	1920
314	EAST	HIGH	1900
402	EAST	HIGH	1900
409	EAST	HIGH	1905
510	EAST	HIGH	1900
518	EAST	HIGH	1900
611	WEST	HIGH	1950
615	EAST	HIGH	1900
615	WEST	HIGH	1955
621	EAST	HIGH	1935
703	EAST	HIGH	1929
709	EAST	HIGH	1914
715	WEST	HIGH	1950
741	WEST	HIGH	1950
218 & 220	WEST	HIGH	1940
110	NORTH	ILLINOIS	1900
204	WEST	ILLINOIS	1884
206	WEST	ILLINOIS	1946
304	WEST	ILLINOIS	1879
310	WEST	ILLINOIS	1904
311	WEST	ILLINOIS	1894
312	WEST	ILLINOIS	N/A
610	EAST	ILLINOIS	1884
116	NORTH	KINNEY	1904
121	SOUTH	KINNEY	1900
207	SOUTH	KINNEY	1914
210	NORTH	KINNEY	1935
211	NORTH	KINNEY	1910
216	SOUTH	KINNEY	1898
228	NORTH	KINNEY	N/A
305	NORTH	KINNEY	1930

311	SOUTH	KINNEY	1914
407	SOUTH	KINNEY	1879
414	SOUTH	KINNEY	1900
421	SOUTH	KINNEY	1939
425	SOUTH	KINNEY	1901
504	SOUTH	KINNEY	1918
505	SOUTH	KINNEY	1918
515	SOUTH	KINNEY	1918
605	SOUTH	KINNEY	1941
608	SOUTH	KINNEY	1900
622	SOUTH	KINNEY	1930
628	SOUTH	KINNEY	1920
814	SOUTH	KINNEY	1938
906	SOUTH	KINNEY	1937
1002	SOUTH	KINNEY	1936
1004	SOUTH	KINNEY	1919
1005	SOUTH	KINNEY	1940
1006	SOUTH	KINNEY	1920
1008	SOUTH	KINNEY	1919
1025	SOUTH	KINNEY	1942
1043	SOUTH	KINNEY	1950
1103	SOUTH	KINNEY	1910
1115	SOUTH	KINNEY	1948
111	SOUTH	LANSING	N/A
114	NORTH	LANSING	1904
219	NORTH	LANSING	1900
307	SOUTH	LANSING	1884
312	NORTH	LANSING	1894
315	NORTH	LANSING	1914
320	NORTH	LANSING	1951
325	NORTH	LANSING	1894
403	NORTH	LANSING	1884
408	SOUTH	LANSING	1982
414	SOUTH	LANSING	1909
415	NORTH	LANSING	1884
415	SOUTH	LANSING	1884

416	NORTH	LANSING	1884
423	NORTH	LANSING	1879
425	SOUTH	LANSING	1900
503	NORTH	LANSING	1880
507	NORTH	LANSING	1884
508	NORTH	LANSING	1885
511	NORTH	LANSING	1924
606	SOUTH	LANSING	1946
621	SOUTH	LANSING	1920
624	NORTH	LANSING	1890
625	SOUTH	LANSING	1890
629	SOUTH	LANSING	1900
636	SOUTH	LANSING	1915
814	NORTH	LANSING	1900
922	NORTH	LANSING	1930
1115	NORTH	LANSING	1905
1210	NORTH	LANSING	1935
201	EAST	LINCOLN	1889
304	EAST	LINCOLN	1910
305	EAST	LINCOLN	1928
312	EAST	LINCOLN	N/A
401	EAST	LINCOLN	1938
521	EAST	LINCOLN	1950
619	EAST	LINCOLN	1934
701	EAST	LINCOLN	N/A
201	EAST	LOCUST	1890
203	EAST	LOCUST	1884
210	EAST	LOCUST	1875
212	EAST	LOCUST	1886
212	WEST	LOCUST	1876
215	EAST	LOCUST	1940
216	EAST	LOCUST	1875
216	WEST	LOCUST	1875
219	EAST	LOCUST	1904
220	EAST	LOCUST	1900
221	WEST	LOCUST	1910

304	EAST	LOCUST	1928
309	EAST	LOCUST	1924
319	WEST	LOCUST	1894
416	WEST	LOCUST	1878
508	EAST	LOCUST	1941
649	EAST	LOCUST	1939
700	EAST	LOCUST	1915
707	EAST	LOCUST	1920
300	SOUTH	MAIN	N/A
303	NORTH	MAIN	1894
309	NORTH	MAIN	1884
401	SOUTH	MAIN	?
401	SOUTH	MAIN	N/A
422	NORTH	MAIN	1887
422	NORTH	MAIN	1889
431	SOUTH	MAIN	1900
500	SOUTH	MAIN	1879
500	SOUTH	MAIN	1889
510	SOUTH	MAIN	1889
510	SOUTH	MAIN	1900
515	SOUTH	MAIN	1874
602	SOUTH	MAIN	1879
602	SOUTH	MAIN	1940
608	SOUTH	MAIN	1890
610	SOUTH	MAIN	1925
620	NORTH	MAIN	?
620	NORTH	MAIN	N/A
708	NORTH	MAIN	1900
708	SOUTH	MAIN	
816	SOUTH	MAIN	1904
900	SOUTH	MAIN	1894
902	SOUTH	MAIN	1920
1002	SOUTH	MAIN	1904
1011	SOUTH	MAIN	1911
1014	SOUTH	MAIN	1900
1016	SOUTH	MAIN	1904

1018	SOUTH	MAIN	1940
1020	SOUTH	MAIN	1874
1022	SOUTH	MAIN	1904
1030	SOUTH	MAIN	1904
103	WEST	MAPLE	1894
203	WEST	MAPLE	1920
205	WEST	MAPLE	N/A
208	EAST	MAPLE	1919
301	WEST	MAPLE	1896
309	WEST	MAPLE	1923
310	EAST	MAPLE	1929
314	WEST	MAPLE	1891
321	WEST	MAPLE	1874
401	EAST	MAPLE	1884
401	WEST	MAPLE	1880
420	WEST	MAPLE	1884
513	EAST	MAPLE	1957
614	EAST	MAPLE	1928
615	EAST	MAPLE	1940
624	EAST	MAPLE	1915
701	EAST	MAPLE	N/A
421 & 423	WEST	MAPLE	1964
104	EAST	MAY	N/A
107	EAST	MAY	N/A
209	WEST	MICHIGAN	1890
301	WEST	MICHIGAN	1879
307	EAST	MICHIGAN	N/A
401	EAST	MICHIGAN	1874
408	EAST	MICHIGAN	1912
505	EAST	MICHIGAN	1919
512	EAST	MICHIGAN	N/A
620	EAST	MICHIGAN	1884
625	EAST	MICHIGAN	1905
701	EAST	MICHIGAN	1894
702	EAST	MICHIGAN	1977
713	EAST	MICHIGAN	1894

213	SOUTH	MILL	N/A
524	EAST	MOSHER	N/A
614	EAST	MOSHER	N/A
110	SOUTH	OAK	N/A
116	SOUTH	OAK	1920
220	SOUTH	OAK	1910
409	SOUTH	OAK	1934
413	SOUTH	OAK	1934
211	EAST	PALMER	1938
215	EAST	PALMER	1900
301	EAST	PALMER	1904
315	EAST	PALMER	1900
322	EAST	PALMER	1904
401	EAST	PALMER	1904
517	EAST	PALMER	1925
611	EAST	PALMER	1935
625	EAST	PALMER	1900
122	EAST	PICKARD	1894
322	EAST	PICKARD	1890
221	SOUTH	PINE	1904
314	SOUTH	PINE	1879
317	SOUTH	PINE	1879
415	SOUTH	PINE	1930
421	SOUTH	PINE	1929
425	SOUTH	PINE	1927
621	SOUTH	PINE	1926
407	SOUTH	PINE GARDEN	N/A
804	SOUTH	PLEASANT	1951
808	SOUTH	PLEASANT	1949
300	SOUTH	UNIVERSITY	1891
310	NORTH	UNIVERSITY	1889
314	NORTH	UNIVERSITY	1884
319	SOUTH	UNIVERSITY	1884
322	NORTH	UNIVERSITY	1879
401	NORTH	UNIVERSITY	1929
403	NORTH	UNIVERSITY	1924

404	NORTH	UNIVERSITY	1929
414	SOUTH	UNIVERSITY	1900
415	NORTH	UNIVERSITY	1904
416	SOUTH	UNIVERSITY	1884
422	NORTH	UNIVERSITY	1874
425	SOUTH	UNIVERSITY	1884
501	SOUTH	UNIVERSITY	1900
507	SOUTH	UNIVERSITY	1904
508	NORTH	UNIVERSITY	1879
515	NORTH	UNIVERSITY	1889
603	NORTH	UNIVERSITY	1900
607	SOUTH	UNIVERSITY	1885
609	SOUTH	UNIVERSITY	1900
621	SOUTH	UNIVERSITY	1900
707	SOUTH	UNIVERSITY	1900
810	SOUTH	UNIVERSITY	1905
812	SOUTH	UNIVERSITY	1908
815	SOUTH	UNIVERSITY	1900
905	SOUTH	UNIVERSITY	1900
909	SOUTH	UNIVERSITY	1900
915	SOUTH	UNIVERSITY	1935
1000	SOUTH	UNIVERSITY	1915
1001	SOUTH	UNIVERSITY	1895
1003	SOUTH	UNIVERSITY	1900
1004	SOUTH	UNIVERSITY	1900
1005	SOUTH	UNIVERSITY	1905
1007	SOUTH	UNIVERSITY	1905
1009	SOUTH	UNIVERSITY	1885
1014	SOUTH	UNIVERSITY	1910
1015	SOUTH	UNIVERSITY	1917
1016	SOUTH	UNIVERSITY	1910
1017	SOUTH	UNIVERSITY	1938
1018	SOUTH	UNIVERSITY	1917
1023	SOUTH	UNIVERSITY	N/A
409	WEST	WALNUT	N/A
412	SOUTH	WASHINGTON	1918

417	SOUTH	WASHINGTON	1879
422	SOUTH	WASHINGTON	1879
423	SOUTH	WASHINGTON	1884
425	SOUTH	WASHINGTON	1924
426	SOUTH	WASHINGTON	1894
430	SOUTH	WASHINGTON	1936
433	SOUTH	WASHINGTON	1874
434	SOUTH	WASHINGTON	1900
518	SOUTH	WASHINGTON	N/A
600	SOUTH	WASHINGTON	1920
601	NORTH	WASHINGTON	1930
607	SOUTH	WASHINGTON	1916
610	SOUTH	WASHINGTON	1924
612	SOUTH	WASHINGTON	1928
615	SOUTH	WASHINGTON	1900
623	NORTH	WASHINGTON	1992
623	SOUTH	WASHINGTON	1992
624	SOUTH	WASHINGTON	1874
630	SOUTH	WASHINGTON	1897
700	SOUTH	WASHINGTON	1900
701	SOUTH	WASHINGTON	1900
714	SOUTH	WASHINGTON	1900
1011	SOUTH	WASHINGTON	1934
1015	SOUTH	WASHINGTON	1894
800	SOUTH	WATSON	1935
901	SOUTH	WATSON	1954
902	SOUTH	WATSON	1962
218	EAST	WISCONSIN	1909
304	EAST	WISCONSIN	1904
315	EAST	WISCONSIN	1879
316	EAST	WISCONSIN	1884
320	EAST	WISCONSIN	1884
321	EAST	WISCONSIN	1884
400	EAST	WISCONSIN	1900
409	EAST	WISCONSIN	1884
510	EAST	WISCONSIN	1914

524	EAST	WISCONSIN	1894
604	EAST	WISCONSIN	1937
610	EAST	WISCONSIN	1911
612	EAST	WISCONSIN	1920
615	EAST	WISCONSIN	1914
701	EAST	WISCONSIN	1909
707	EAST	WISCONSIN	1986
708	EAST	WISCONSIN	1910
715	EAST	WISCONSIN	1924
511	EAST	WOODWORTH	1945

Photo Credits

BARBARA BARBERI,
ROBERT BANTA
LARRY BOURSAW
BILL CAIN
CLARKE HISTORICAL LIBRARY, Park Library Building, Central Michigan University, Mt. Pleasant Campus
COLLEEN CAMPBELL
CATHERINE COTTON
JOHN CUMMING
KAREN DAY, Clare, Michigan
RITA DENI
PAUL ELLIOTT
"ROSIE" FUNNELL
MIKE GEORGIA
MARY HARPER
BRIGID HINKLEY
HUDSON KEENAN
NORMAN X. LYON COLLECTION, Clarke Historical Library:
RANDY MARTIN
JOYCE McCLAIN
GAIL McDONALD
WILLIAM McEWAN photos courtesy SHERRY SPONSELLER
GRETCHEN MERRILL
MICHIGAN OIL & GAS NEWS
MI OIL & GAS NEWS COLLECTION, Clarke Historical Library, CMU, Mt. Pleasant Campus
MT. PLEASANT (MICHIGAN) AREA HISTORICAL SOCIETY; ALAN SHINAVAR photos courtesy SHERRY SPONSELLER;
JOAN MOSES
JACK NEYER
STAN & JOYCE PRIDGEON
MARY ELLEN & HARRY RUARK,
DICK AND SUSAN HARPER SWITZER
SHARON SCHMITT
SHERRY SPONSELLER
GERALD & MARGARET TRAVIS
PAT WILMOT
SALLY WOJCIECHOWSKI
VALERIE WOLTERS
SANDRA HOWARD WOOD, 708 South University

Unless otherwise noted, all of the people credited here are from Mt. Pleasant, MI
Apologies with anyone accidently forgotten.

Bibliography

Portrait and Biographical Album, Isabella County Michigan. Chicago IL; Chapman Brothers, 1884.

Child, Gerald Dwight, Sr., The Campbell Building, Genealogical Society of Isabella County, Mt. Pleasant MI 1999.

Clarke Historical Library, Park Library, *Archives*, Central Michigan University, Mt. Pleasant MI campus.

Cumming, John. *The First 100 Years; A Portrait of Central Michigan University 1892-1992.*Mount Pleasant, MI; Central Michigan University Press, 1992.

Cumming, John. *This Place Mount Pleasant.* Mt. Pleasant, MI; Central Michigan University Press, 1989.

Fancher, Isaac A. *Past and Present of Isabella County Michigan.* Indianapolis IN; B. F. Bowen & Company, 1911.

Isabella County Genealogical Society. *Isabella County, Michigan, Families and History.* Paducah KY; Turner Publishing, 2003.

McAlester, Virginia and Lee. *A Field Guide to American Houses,* New York: Alfred A. Knoph 2011

Miller, H. A. and Charles J, Seely. *Faces and Places Familiar.* Mt Pleasant MI Courier Press, 1906.

Numerous websites, newspapers and special events brochures.

Shepherd Historical Society. *Isabella County 1982.* Dallas TX; Taylor Publishing, 1982.

Westbrook, Jack R.. *Central Michigan University.* Mt. Pleasant SC, Arcadia Publushing, 2007

Westbrook, Jack R.. *The BIG Picture Book of Mt. Pleasant Michigany.* Mt. Pleasant MI, ORSB Publushing, 2010.

.

About the Author

JACK R. WESTBROOK is a Mt. Pleasant, Michigan, resident, retired Managing Editor of the Michigan Oil & Gas News magazine and author of seven previous historical photo review books four books were with Arcadia Publishing Company: *MICHIGAN OIL & GAS; MT. PLEASANT (Michigan) THEN AND NOW; CENTRAL MICHIGAN UNIVERSITY*; *ISABELLA COUNTY (Michigan) 1859-2009. Three additional books have been self-published by ORSB Publishing: YESTERDAY'S SCHOOL KIDS OF ISABELLA COUNTY* with co-author historian/genealogist Sherry Sponseller*; THE BIG PICTURE BOOK OF MT. PLEASANT, MICHIGAN;* and *Michigan natural resources trust fund: 1976-2011, 1ST and 2nd Editions*

Additionally, Westbrook was publication preparation consultant for three autobiographical books: *DIAMONDS ON THE WATER*, an autobiographical collection of fishing trip stories by Dr. Roy Burlington: *ALMOST A CATTLE BARON* by William J. Strickler; and *ANOINTED WITH OIL* by C. John Miller.

He is a frequent public speaker on the subjects of each of his books.

www.ingramcontent.com/pod-product-compliance
Lightning Source LLC
LaVergne TN
LVHW050616100826
845148LV00011B/1613

* 9 7 8 0 9 8 4 0 3 6 1 1 0 *